RECIPES FROM HISTORIC
Louisiana

RECIPES FROM HISTORIC
Louisiana

COOKING WITH LOUISIANA'S FINEST RESTAURANTS

LINDA & STEVE BAUER

BRIGHT SKY PRESS

BRIGHT SKY PRESS

Box 416
Albany, Texas 76430

10   9   8   7   6   5   4   3   2   1

Bauer, Linda.
Recipes from historic Louisiana / by Linda and Steve Bauer.
p. cm.
ISBN 1-931721-72-6 (alk. paper)
1. Cookery, American—Louisiana style. I. Bauer, Steve, 1943– II. Title.

TX715.B349225 2006
641.57763—dc22

2005045693

Book and cover design by Isabel Lasater Hernandez

Printed in China through Asia Pacific Offset

Other books by the Authors

The American Sampler Cookbook

At Ease in the White House

The New American Sampler Cookbook

How to Do Business with the Federal Government

Recipes from Historic Texas

The Great American Sampler Cookbook

The Homeschool Handbook

*This book is dedicated to those who love the great state of
Louisiana and want to see it rise again to new heights of culinary
and historic significance. Most of all, we want to remember those
who lost their lives, homes, businesses, family members, or friends.*

*We thank the many volunteers, workers, and supporters
throughout the world who have selflessly contributed and labored
to help the state recover and regain its unique place in our nation.*

May God bless each and every one of you!

Contents

Introduction

The name "Louisiana" summons up some very evocative images, and many of them have to do with food: Moss-draped live oaks and fragrant magnolias. *Gumbo.* White-columned porticos and lacy cast-iron galleries. *Beignets and chicory-laced coffee.* Lazy-flowing bayous and the mighty Mississippi. *Pralines.* Jazz and zydeco. *Crawfish étouffée.* Mardi Gras. *Red beans and rice.*

Louisianans have long known that good food is an essential element of the rich cultural heritage that makes their state unique, and this collection of recipes shows why. What makes these dishes particularly appealing (apart from their mouth-watering goodness, of course) is the fact that they are gathered from places that are themselves significant pieces of Louisiana's treasured legacy from the past. These places—from antebellum plantations that have sheltered generations of local families to modest storefront cafés and elegant restaurants that have served generations of diners—remind us how important it is to protect our heritage so that we can live with it, learn from it, and celebrate it.

Sadly, in 2005 Louisiana's heritage took a real beating from Hurricanes Katrina and Rita. As this is being written, the National Trust and our preservation partners are working to ensure that damaged historic buildings are not needlessly demolished and that flooded historic neighborhoods are made livable again without sacrificing their character. It is an enormously challenging task, but we are committed to doing it right. If we don't, Louisiana could lose part of what makes it special—and America could lose part of its heart and soul.

What high wind and high water did to the historic places of Louisiana is a powerful reminder that our heritage is perilously fragile—and that saving it is not someone else's job. As you savor the dishes presented in this book, take a moment to recognize the restaurants where they originated as important cultural links with the past. Then take a moment to figure out how you can help keep the past alive in your own hometown.

Richard Moe, President
National Trust for Historic Preservation

17

GREATER NEW ORLEANS

For most people, Louisiana means New Orleans—home of Mardi Gras, great Cajun food, and, of course, the French Quarter. But the 40-day celebration culminating in "Fat Tuesday," the day before Ash Wednesday and the start of Lent, is only part of the story of this fabulous party town. There is so much more to see and do, people flock to the city year-round.

Attracted by moderate temperature swings, tourists visit the Audubon Park zoo, the aquarium, more than a dozen museums and art centers, a dozen golf courses, and several professional sports enterprises. There are also 19 universities to attract students as well as alumni and visitors.

Undoubtedly, New Orleans' main attraction is food. Virtually every kind of cuisine is available, with the preponderance including either seafood or Cajun origins, or both. The French Quarter—the original settlement and oldest part of the city—contains a myriad of very fine eating establishments, as you will discover when you read on, and there hasn't been a vacant lot there for decades.

A number of great restaurants are also located throughout the city, and we strongly encourage you to enjoy not only Bourbon Street and the Vieux Carré (French Quarter), but also to extend your investigation to the surrounding areas and take in the whole of the city. You will discover that the spirit of the people of New Orleans will survive any storm.

Antoine's Restaurant

Antoine's Restaurant
713–717 Rue St. Louis
New Orleans, Louisiana 70130
(504) 581-4422
www.antoines.com

Established in 1840, Antoine's is the country's oldest family-run restaurant. It was spring in 1840: New Orleans was queen city of the Mississippi River, cotton was king and French gentlemen settled their differences under the oaks with pistols for two and coffee for one. "Dixie," the song destined to become the marching anthem for Confederate forces in the War Between the States, had not yet been written.

This was the city young Antoine Alciatore adopted, after two frustrating years in New York, to establish a restaurant that would endure under his family's direction for more than 150 years and set the standard that has made New Orleans one of the great dining centers of the world.

It was on St. Louis Street, just one block from the spot the famed restaurant occupies today, that the 27-year-old Alciatore started "Antoine's," a name that would become synonymous with fine food. He felt at home in the French-speaking city of extravagant lordly aristocrats, an ideal audience for his culinary artistry.

After a brief period in the kitchen of the grand St. Charles Hotel, Antoine opened a pension, a boarding house, and a restaurant. It wasn't long before the fragrances wafting from his kitchen brought New Orleans to his door and, in five years, the Pension Alciatore was firmly established.

It was then that he made arrangements for his fiancée to join him from New York. She came to New Orleans with her sister and she and Antoine were married. Together they worked to build up their pension with culinary emphasis. New Orleans' gentility was so taken with the restaurant that it soon outgrew its small quarters. Antoine's moved down the block and then eventually, in 1868, to the spot on St. Louis Street where the restaurant stands today.

In 1874, Antoine fell ill and took leave of his family, placing management of the restaurant in his wife's hands. He felt he had not much longer to live and wished to die and be buried in his birthplace in France. He told his wife he did not want her to watch him decline and said as he left, "As I take the boat for Marseilles, we will not meet again on earth." He died within the year.

Jules served as apprentice under his mother's tutelage for six years before she sent him to France, where he worked in the great kitchens of Paris, Strassburg, and Marseilles. He returned to New Orleans and became chef of the famous Pickwick Club in 1887 before his mother summoned him to head the house of Antoine.

His genius was in the kitchen, where he invented Oysters Rockefeller, so named for the richness of the sauce. They stand as one of the great culinary creations of all time and that recipe remains a closely-guarded Antoine's secret—though it has been imitated countless times.

Jules married Althea Roy, daughter of a planter in Youngsville, Louisiana, and Marie Louise, the grand dame of the family, was born. A son, Roy Louis, was born in 1902 and headed the restaurant for almost 40 years until his death in 1972.

Marie Louise married William Guste, and their sons, William Jr., former attorney general of Louisiana, and Roy Sr., became the fourth generation of the family to head the restaurant. In 1975, Roy's son, Roy Jr., became proprietor and served until 1984. He was followed by William's son, Bernard "Randy" Guste.

The long line of the Alciatore-Guste family members has guided Antoine's to continued greatness—through the War

"When you want real food go to Antoine's, when you want real life go to New Orleans."
Herbert Hoover

Between the States, two World Wars, Prohibition, and the Great Depression.

Countless celebrities have dined at Antoine's. Lining the walls are photographs of the rich and famous who have feasted amid the splendor: musicians, politicians, military personnel, sports figures, royalty—the list is endless. It includes Franklin Roosevelt, Calvin Coolidge, Herbert Hoover, Bob Hope, Rex Harrison, Al Jolson, Pope John Paul II, and Bing Crosby, to name just a few.

The names of each of the dining rooms at Antoine's are steeped in history. Mardi Gras has been the premier attraction in

New Orleans since 1857, just a few years after the birth of Antoine's. Four of the restaurant's private rooms bear the names of the family's Carnival krewes: Rex, Proteus, Hermes, and 12th Night Revelers.

Roy Alciatore, Antoine's proprietor for nearly 40 years, created the Rex Room in recognition of "The Krewe Of Rex"—its King reigns over the Mardi Gras celebration. A photo of the Duke and Duchess of Windsor is exhibited outside the Rex Room. The couple dined at Antoine's during Mardi Gras of 1949.

The vast, glistening main dining room is located just past the first dining room at the entrance, and is named the Large Annex. It has been a local favorite for decades. Many New Orleans families have had the same waiter for years.

The Japanese Room was designed with Oriental motifs popular at the turn of the century, including hand-painted walls and ceilings. Many large banquets were held there until December 7, 1941, when the Japanese bombed Pearl Harbor, ushering the United States into World War II. Roy Alciatore then closed the room, and it remained that way for 43 years. It was reopened in 1984 and brought back to its original splendor with beautiful hand-painted wallpaper in the design of a rose trellis.

The Roy Alciatore Room was formerly the Capitol Room, so named because the wooden panels on the walls were taken from the old capitol building in Baton Rouge. This room has a twin next door, Maison Verte. Both rooms are almost identical in size and decor, with lush deep-pile green carpets and four black marble fireplaces, two in each room.

The Mystery Room acquired its name due to Prohibition, the 18th Amendment prohibiting the sale of alcoholic drinks (from 1919 until 1933). During this time, some would go through a door in the ladies' restroom to a secret room and exit with a coffee cup full of booze (in spite of the Blue Laws).The protocol phrase at table when asked from whence it came was: "It's a mystery to me." The name stuck and, to this day, it's still the Mystery Room, nestled charmingly at the end of an interesting corridor. The room is dotted with souvenirs from famous restaurants around the world, including Groucho Marx's beret.

The 1840 Room, fashioned in the style of the period, is a charming salon for dining. Photographs of successive generations of the Alciatore family also decorate the room and add to the richness of the warm, red interior. It replicates a fashionable dining room from that time and is also a museum of sorts, housing a Parisian cookbook circa 1659, and the restaurant's silver duck press, among other treasures.

CREOLE GUMBO

Serves 6

¾ stick butter

2 cups green onion, chopped

2 cups okra, sliced

1 cup white onion, chopped

2 cups raw shrimp, peeled

2 cups raw oysters

1 cup tomato pulp, chopped

2 cups tomato juice

1½ quarts fish stock

3 crabs (top shell discarded, cut into 4 pieces)

3 tablespoons flour

1 tablespoon filé (sassafras)

3 cups cooked rice

Salt, pepper, and cayenne to taste

Melt the butter and sauté the green onion, okra, white onion, and crab.

In a separate pot, put the shrimp, oysters, tomatoes, and tomato juice with 1½ quarts of fish stock and bring to a boil. Let boil for a minute, then add to the first pot.

In a small skillet, cook the butter and flour together until brown. Blend this brown roux with the filé and some of the gumbo liquid and add to the gumbo. Add salt and pepper and cayenne to taste. Simmer for 1½ hours.

To serve, pour 1½ cups of gumbo into each bowl over ½ cup rice.

The Bouillabaisse of Louisiana appears in many forms. Ours is the classic Creole seafood gumbo.

Café Du Monde

Café Du Monde

French Market

800 Decatur Street

New Orleans, Louisiana 70116

(504) 525-4544

The Original Café Du Monde Coffee Stand was established in 1862 in the New Orleans French Market. The Café is open 24 hours a day, seven days a week and closes only on Christmas Day.

Coffee first came to North America by way of New Orleans back in the mid-1700s. It was successfully cultivated in Martinique about 1720. The French brought coffee with them as they began to settle new colonies along the Mississippi.

The taste for coffee with chicory was developed by the French during their civil war. Coffee was scarce during those times, and they found that chicory added body and flavor to the brew. The Acadians from Nova Scotia brought this taste and many other French customs to Louisiana. Chicory is the root of the endive plant. The root of the plant is roasted and ground. It is added to the coffee to soften the bitter edge of the dark-roasted coffee. It adds an almost chocolate flavor to the café au lait served at Café Du Monde.

The Café Du Monde coffee with chicory is traditionally served au lait: half-and-half mixed with hot milk. However, personal preference always prevails. Some like their coffee strong and black, or with sugar; maybe with a little more milk, or maybe a weaker brew. Coffee with chicory should be presented in vacuum bottles to keep the coffee hot and to give the customer the opportunity to experiment with their personal preference.

The Original Café Du Monde is a traditional coffee shop. Its menu consists of dark-roasted coffee with chicory, white and chocolate milk, fresh-squeezed orange juice, and beignets—square French-style doughnuts, lavishly covered with powdered sugar. In 1988 Iced Coffee was introduced to the cafe.

The following recipes are from the shop across the street from Café du Monde that sells such products such as beignet mix and the famous coffee with chicory.

PROFITEROLES

Yields approximately 36

4 cups flour

2 cups butter

3 ¾ cups milk

15 eggs

Heat butter and milk together. When it boils, add flour. Stir until a ball is formed that does not stick to the side of the pan. Put in a bowl. Add eggs, two at a time at medium speed.

Pipe out on parchment paper. Bake at 350 degrees in convection oven for 30 minutes. Do not open the oven until done. Cool. Split and add ice cream. Top with strawberry or chocolate syrup.

SOUR CREAM POUND CAKE

1 cup butter

2 cups sugar

2 eggs

½ teaspoon vanilla

2 cups cake flour

1 teaspoon baking powder

¼ teaspoon salt

1 cup sour cream

½ cup pecans, chopped

1 ½ teaspoons cinnamon

2 tablespoons sugar

Cream butter, 2 cups of sugar, eggs, and vanilla. In a separate bowl, combine flour, baking powder, and salt. Alternately fold sour cream and dry ingredients into butter mix.

Mix pecans, cinnamon and 2 tablespoons of sugar.

Grease a bundt pan. Pour in half of the mix. Sprinkle with half the pecan mix. Pour in remaining batter and finish with remaining nuts.

Bake at 350 degrees for 55 minutes.

25

PEACHES PATTY ANN

Yields 1 pint sauce

12-ounce can peaches
1 tablespoon cinnamon
½ teaspoon nutmeg
4 ounces (1 stick) butter
½ cup sugar
2 ounces peach schnapps or peach liqueur
Ice cream

Melt the butter and add sugar, cooking for 3 minutes. Strain peaches from juice and set peaches aside. Combine peach juice with melted butter and sugar, and simmer for 1 minute. Add cinnamon, nutmeg, and peaches. Simmer for 2 minutes. Add peach liqueur and serve over vanilla ice cream.

LOUISIANA PRALINES

Yields 20–30

1 pound dark brown sugar
1 cup granulated sugar
½ teaspoon salt
¾ cup milk
2–3 cups whole pecan halves
2 tablespoons butter
½ teaspoon vanilla

Cook sugars, salt, and milk until temperature reaches 238 degrees or the mixture forms a soft ball. Add pecans and bring to a rolling boil. Remove mixture and add vanilla and butter. Let stand in the saucepan for 20 minutes.

Spread wax or parchment paper on table. Beat mix slightly until it glosses. Drop by spoonfuls onto paper. Cool 20 minutes and wrap individually in plastic.

KING CAKE
USING MAM PAPAUL'S KING CAKE KIT

Serves 12

Mam Papaul's King Cake Kit
1 egg
1 cup warm water
$^1/_2$ cup margarine
2 tablespoons melted butter
Brown sugar praline mix

*On learning that coffee was considered a slow poison,
"I think it must be so, for I have been drinking it
for sixty-five years and I am not dead yet."*
Voltaire

Mix and knead in bag as follows: Place cake mix (large bag) and yeast in large re-closable bag. Lock re-closable bag and shake vigorously. Add water and margarine. Lock bag. With fingers outside bag, mix by squeezing and pulling dough until margarine can no longer be seen. Add egg. Press air from bag and lock. With fingers on outside of bag, mix and knead ingredients by squeezing and pulling dough for approximately 12 minutes. Be careful not to puncture bag.

Unlock bag. Set bag of dough in a bowl in a warm place for 15 minutes. (Warm Place Hint: turn oven on lowest setting for 2 minutes *only*. Then turn oven off. Place bag of dough inside)

Place dough on lightly floured surface. Flour rolling pin and roll dough into a 5-inch by 30-inch rectangle.

Mix melted butter and brown sugar praline mix in a small bowl. Add nuts if desired. Spread evenly on dough. From 30-inch side, roll dough jellyroll fashion. Pinch ends to seal. Place on large cookie sheet. Shape into an oval. Let rise in a warm place approximately 30 minutes or until dough doubles in size.

Bake in a preheated oven at 375 degrees for 20–25 minutes or until nicely browned. Cool.

Mix 1 tablespoon of water and white glaze mix in a small bowl. Spread over cooled cake. Decorate with Mardi Gras crystals. Place golden baby under cake.

Royal Sonesta Hotel

Long before the name Sonesta became synonymous with quality hotels, a prize-winning dairy farm in Holliston, Massachusetts, was named "Sonesta Farms" after its owners, Abraham (nicknamed Sonny) and Ester Sonnabend.

Sonny was an entrepreneur who purchased financially troubled companies for tax purposes, made them successful, and sold them at a profit. It was not until 1943 that Sonny (known as A.M. Sonnabend in business circles), at the age of 49, became involved in hotels as a real estate investment.

The first hotel acquisition for A.M. (and six other partners) was the Preston Beach Hotel on the north shore of Boston. Because of his business knowledge, A.M. was put in charge of managing the hotels. They became known as Sonnabend-operated hotels. By the 1950s, there were four Sonnabend-operated hotels, including the world-famous Plaza in New York.

A.M.'s sons—Roger, Paul, and Steven—have made the hotel business their lives' work; many of their children, who now encompass the third generation of Sonnabends, are also dedicated to achieving excellence in the hospitality industry.

The Sonnabends were introduced to the Royal Sonesta Hotel New Orleans' prime location on Bourbon Street by the developer of the nearby Royal Orleans Hotel. The Royal Sonesta opened in September of 1969 and has since become a landmark on Bourbon Street in the heart of the historic French Quarter.

The site of this grand hotel enjoys a long and colorful history that dates back to 1721. That year, French military engineer Adrien de Pauger first laid out the city of Nouvelle Orleans, or New Orleans. The block of land where the hotel now stands was originally comprised of 12 lots made up of houses, stables, gardens, courtyards, and carriageways.

Among the notable residents were a philanthropist, a statesman, the first postmaster of New Orleans, and a Shakespearean actor. Many different commercial enterprises operated on the site over the years as well: a costume shop, a bakery, an herb garden, a vinegar factory, and a winery. The American

Royal Sonesta Hotel

300 Bourbon Street

New Orleans, Louisiana 70130

(504) 586-0300

Brewing Company, makers of the popular Regal Beer, purchased the winery in 1890.

Little evidence of the brewery remained in 1964 after demolition of this large group of old buildings. Three years later, construction began on the $16 million Royal Sonesta Hotel. Local jazz great Sweet Emma cut the ribbon at the hotel's grand opening.

In its early years, the Royal Sonesta housed Economy Hall, a popular jazz club where local greats such as Fats Domino and Louis Prima used to perform. Years later, the current site of the Sales and Catering Office housed the New Orleans Jazz Museum (which has since relocated to the old U.S. Mint building and is home to such memorabilia as Louis Armstrong's cornet.)

The exterior of the hotel was designed to look like a group of typical 1830s New Orleans row houses, a unique architectural style in the French Quarter. Inside this oasis on Bourbon Street, public areas are elegantly appointed with crystal, marble, bronze, and traditional furnishings. Many of the 500 guest rooms and suites have French doors that open onto a terrace or balcony surrounding the quiet, tropical courtyard.

The hotel's Old World style—combined with its modern-day amenities and personal service—continues to attract locals and visitors year after year who seek the ultimate New Orleans experience. The Royal Sonesta Hotel is dedicated to preserving the rich heritage of the historic French Quarter neighborhood in which it resides.

Begue's Restaurant is named after Elizabeth Begue, a restaurateur who lived in the 1800s and whom many New Orleanians credit with the invention of the Sunday brunch concept and the Po' Boy sandwich (see page 31). Today Begue's overlooks a lush, tropical courtyard in the Royal Sonesta Hotel.

CRÊPES SUZETTE

Yields 10–15 crêpes

12 crêpes (recipe follows)
$1/2$ cup sugar
1 orange
$1/2$ lemon
$1/4$ cup butter
$1/8$ cup orange liqueur
$1/4$ cup cognac

In a flambé pan, heat the sugar until it melts and begins to caramelize.

Cut several strips of rind from the orange and one from the lemon, and add them to the pan. Add the butter and squeeze the juice from the orange and lemon into the pan. Stir until the sugar is dissolved and the mixture is a little syrupy.

Add the orange liqueur. One by one, dip the crêpes in the sauce to coat them, then fold them into quarters in the pan. Add the cognac and allow it to heat for a few seconds.

Flame the cognac by carefully tipping the pan toward the burner flame until the cognac ignites. Shake the pan gently and spoon the sauce over the crêpes until the flame dies down.

Serve three crêpes per portion, spooning some of the remaining sauce over each serving.

Crêpes

2 eggs
$1/8$ teaspoon salt
1 cup flour
1 cup milk
$1/4$ cup melted butter

Put all the ingredients in a blender. Blend for 1 minute. Scrape down the sides, blend for another 20 seconds.

Refrigerate batter for at least 1 hour.

Cook crêpes in a pan at medium-high heat. Use about 2–3 tablespoons batter per crêpe. Pour into the pan and immediately swirl the pan around so the batter coats the bottom. (Crêpe size should be about 8 inches.) Cook for about 30–45 seconds, flip and cook for about 10 more seconds.

Chef's note: Crêpes Suzette go perfectly with champagne on a romantic evening!

PO' BOY

According to some accounts, this sandwich was created by a Mme. Begue, owner of a coffee stall in New Orleans' Old French Market, in 1895. She took a long, thin loaf of French bread, slit it in half lengthwise, buttered it generously, sliced it in thirds or fourths (not cutting through the bottom crust) and put a different filling into each section. The name is said to derive from the pleas of hungry black youths who begged, "Please give a sandwich to a po' boy."

The generally accepted history is that the Po' Boy sandwich was invented by two brothers, Clovis and Benjamin Martin, in 1929 at their restaurant in the French Market. It is said, true or not, that this sandwich extravaganza began during a local transit worker's strike. The two brothers took pity on those "poor boys" and began offering sandwiches made from leftovers to any workers who came to their restaurant's back door at the end of the day. For five cents, a striker could buy a sandwich filled with gravy and trimmings (end pieces from beef roasts) or gravy and sliced potatoes.

15 shrimp (50–60 count)
1 9-inch loaf French bread
3 tomatoes, sliced
2 tablespoons mayonnaise
1 pickle spear
2 wedges lemon

Fry the shrimp in oil.
Slit the bread in half lengthwise.
Spread the mayonnaise on the bread. Fill with shrimp and cut into thirds or in half.
Serve with pickle spear and lemon wedge.

CAJUN POTATO SALAD

Serves 1–2
1 Yukon Gold potato
$1/2$ hard boiled egg
1 tablespoon mayonnaise
$1/4$ red onion, chopped
1 teaspoon Cajun spices
1 teaspoon garlic, chopped
1 teaspoon sweet relish
Salt and pepper

Boil the potato, then smash and mix with the rest of the ingredients and serve in a cup.

K-Paul's Louisiana Kitchen

K-Paul's Louisiana Kitchen

416 Chartres Street

New Orleans, Louisiana 70130

(504) 596-2530

www.kpauls.com

When Chef Paul Prudhomme and his late wife, K, opened their modest 62-seat K-Paul's Louisiana Kitchen in 1979, they had no idea the restaurant was soon to become an overnight sensation, with nightly lines of eager diners waiting sometimes hours to be seated. That was back in the days when K-Paul's didn't accept reservations. But now, under the hands-on direction of Chef Paul Prudhomme and Chef Paul Miller, the restaurant has gone through major changes to keep up with the growing demands of its clients.

Based on the designs of the original 1834 structure, K-Paul's was extensively refurbished and expanded in 1996 and now offers seating for more than 200 guests. Dining areas include balcony dining, spacious dining rooms on both the first and second floors, and an intimate courtyard for dining al fresco. K's Parlor, an enclosed private room on the second floor, hosts parties, corporate events, and other special occasions. Both floors feature an open-air kitchen where diners can see exactly how each dish is prepared. K-Paul's gladly accepts reservations and offers catering on-site or anywhere around the world.

Leek, Sun-Dried Tomato, Shiitake Mushroom, and Champagne Soup

Makes 8 cups

2 pounds leeks

$^1/_2$ cup sun-dried tomato pieces

3 tablespoons unsalted butter or margarine

1 cup onions, chopped

1 $^1/_2$ tablespoons Chef Paul Prudhomme's Meat Magic® *or* Vegetable Magic® *or* Magic Seasoning Salt®

4 cups shiitake mushrooms, sliced

$^3/_4$ cup champagne or dry sparkling wine (optional)

2 cups chicken stock (salt-free)

2 cups heavy cream

1 cup Gouda cheese, grated

Trim off the dark green leaves (leaving the white and light green parts) and the root ends of the leeks and discard. Split the remaining white part of the leeks in half lengthwise and wash thoroughly under running water, making sure that all dirt and debris are removed from between the sections. Slice the leek halves crosswise into very thin half rounds. You should have about 3 cups

Soften the sun-dried tomatoes in warm water. When they are soft, drain and cut in small julienne strips.

In a medium-sized pot, melt the margarine over medium-high heat. Add the leeks and onions and cook, stirring frequently, until the onions are wilted and transparent, about 8 minutes.

Add the Magic Seasoning Blend and stir well. Continue to cook until the seasoning begins to darken slightly, about 2 minutes.

Add the shiitake mushrooms and the julienned sun-dried tomatoes. Cook, stirring frequently, until the mushrooms begin to darken, about 4 minutes.

Add ¼ cup of the champagne and stir well, scraping the bottom of the pot to dissolve any browned bits on the bottom. Add the chicken stock. Bring to a boil and simmer over medium-low heat until the flavors of the soup are married, about 20 minutes.

Add the cream, stir well and return to a boil. Simmer until the soup has reduced slightly, about 10 minutes. Gradually add the cheese, stirring constantly until all the cheese has melted and dissolved. Add the remaining champagne and stir briefly. Remove from heat and serve.

Champagne is optional.

33

BRONZED STEAK
WITH A GINGERSNAP GRAVY

Each time we tested this recipe, we used a different brand of gingersnaps. They all had different tastes and thickening properties, so you may need to add a little more or less stock to the sauce to obtain the thickness you want.

Serves 4

Seasoning Mix

3 tablespoons plus 1 teaspoon Chef Paul Prudhomme's Meat Magic® *or* Blackened Steak Magic®, *or* Vegetable Magic®

1 ³/₄ teaspoons ground ginger

1 teaspoon dry mustard

3 tablespoons unsalted butter

1 cup onions, chopped

¹/₂ cup red bell pepper, chopped

¹/₂ cup yellow bell pepper, chopped

1 teaspoon fresh garlic, minced

2 teaspoons fresh ginger, minced

About 2 cups chicken stock (preferred) or vegetable stock (see note above)

1 cup heavy cream

¹/₃ cup gingersnap cookies (preferably dark, good-quality gingersnaps), broken in pieces

4 beef tenderloins (¹/₂-inch thick) or favorite steak

2 tablespoons vegetable oil

Combine the seasoning mix ingredients in a small bowl.

Heat the butter in a 10-inch skillet over high heat. As soon as it melts, stir in 1 tablespoon plus 1 teaspoon of the seasoning mix. When the butter is sizzling and foamy, add the onions and all the bell peppers. Stir well, then cover and cook for 6 minutes.

Uncover, stir, and scrape up any brown bits sticking to the bottom of the skillet. The vegetables will be brightly colored and just beginning to brown. Re-cover and cook for 4 more minutes, stir and scrape again, then re-cover and cook for 2 more minutes. The onions should now be golden brown (edged with dark brown), the bell peppers slightly crunchy, and the flavors of all the ingredients well-defined, with a creamy sweetness at the end.

Stir in the garlic, ginger, and 1 teaspoon of the seasoning mix. Stir well, then add 1 cup of the stock and stir and scrape well until all the browned material is dissolved. The mixture should be a red-brown color. Re-cover and cook for 8 minutes, then whisk in the gingersnaps and the remaining 1 cup of the stock. Cook, whisking frequently, until the mixture is smooth, about 3 minutes.

Gradually whisk in the cream, bring to a boil, then reduce the heat to medium and simmer, whisking frequently, until the gravy has thickened to the consistency of heavy cream, about 10 minutes. The finished sauce should be a rich brown color and the flavor dominated by the ginger flavors—both

Continued next page

fresh and dried—and sweetness of the gingersnap cookies. Makes about 3 cups.

Season both sides of each steak evenly with ½ teaspoon of the seasoning mix.

Place the oil in a 12-inch non-stick skillet over high heat just until the pan is hot, about 3–4 minutes. Place the steaks in the pan and cook, turning once, until they are just cooked through (medium), about 2–3 minutes per side. The steaks are properly cooked when somewhat firm to the touch. Serve immediately, dividing the sauce evenly among the portions.

K-PAUL'S MASHED POTATOES

Serves 6

3 medium- to large-sized potatoes, about 3 pounds, peeled

2 cups heavy cream

2 tablespoons plus ¹⁄₂ teaspoon Chef Paul Prudhomme's Vegetable Magic® or Meat Magic® or Magic Seasoning Salt®

¹⁄₄ pound (1 stick) unsalted butter, melted

Dice 1 potato into 1-inch cubes and the other 2 into ½-inch cubes.

Add enough water to a large pot to measure 1½ inches deep and place over high heat. When the water boils, add the potatoes, cover, and cook until the large-diced potatoes are fork tender, about 20–25 minutes. Drain thoroughly.

While the potatoes are draining, melt the butter in a small skillet, then remove from heat.

Place the drained potatoes in a food processor or mixer and process until smooth (you may have to do this in batches). With the machine running, slowly add the melted butter to the potatoes, and when it is mixed in, add the cream. Process only until the potatoes are stiff but not dry, about 3–4 minutes. When the potatoes reach the right consistency, add the Magic Seasoning Blend and pulse a couple of times, just to mix it in. Do not overmix!

This is the way we make mashed potatoes at K-Paul's, and our customers say they are to die for! Since people are always asking what our secret is, we thought we'd share it with you. If a potato dish can be considered first class, this one definitely is. Some of our regular customers even order it for dessert!

Brennan's

Owen Edward Brennan, the founder of Brennan's Restaurant, was born April 5, 1910, in New Orleans' "Irish Channel" to Owen Patrick Brennan and his wife, Nellie. Over a span of the next twenty-three years, Owen's younger siblings were born in the following order: Adelaide, John, Ella, Richard (Dick) and Dorothy (Dottie).

Owen was already married when Dick and Dottie were born. Shortly after their births, Owen Edward Brennan, Jr. (Pip) was born to Owen and his wife, Maude. In time, Maude gave birth to two more sons, James (Jimmy) and Theodore (Ted), providing Owen with three male heirs.

Throughout his adult life, Owen Edward Brennan was driven by his devotion and an undaunting sense of responsibility to support not only his own wife and three sons but his parents and siblings as well. His father, Owen Patrick Brennan, was a New Orleans foundry laborer, which had made supporting Nellie and their six children very difficult; his eldest son, Owen Edward Brennan set out to make his fortune.

In September of 1943, Owen purchased the Old Absinthe House on Bourbon Street. The Absinthe House had been built in 1798 and was known to be pirate Jean Lafitte's secret hangout. As its most recent proprietor, Owen staged lifelike mannequins of the notorious Lafitte and Andrew Jackson in what he called the "Secret Room"—the very room in which the pact was supposedly made in New Orleans' defense against the British at the Battle of New Orleans.

Owen became one of the city's best-known hosts at his colorful Old Absinthe House, "the oldest saloon in America." Pianist Fats Pichon added to its charm with his talented renditions, from Bach to boogie.

Owen added another dimension of ambience to the historical and musical atmosphere of the Old Absinthe House by inviting myriads of visitors to attach their business cards to its inside walls. Eventually, thousands of cards and autographed papers hung from its ceiling as well.

Owen's customers could recapture the past with a Pirate's Dream, the specialty drink of the Old Absinthe House. He labeled it "the highbrow of all lowbrow drinks." Owen perpetuated the popularity of the Absinthe Frappe, an original

Brennan's

417 Royal Street

New Orleans, Louisiana 70130

(504) 525-9711

36

creation of the Absinthe House and a favorite of Presidents Franklin D. Roosevelt and Dwight D. Eisenhower and Admiral Earnest King.

Owen's good friend, Count Arnaud, whose restaurant was a popular New Orleans dining spot, allegedly posed a challenge to Owen. Owen would relay complaints about other restaurants overheard at the Absinthe House to offending restaurant owners. Count Arnaud told him, "You're forever telling me about the complaints you hear. If you think you can do better, why don't you open a restaurant?"

In July of 1946, Owen Edward Brennan leased the Vieux Carré Restaurant directly across the street from the Old Absinthe House. He named his new restaurant for himself, Owen Brennan's French & Creole Restaurant. With time, it came to be more commonly known as Owen Brennan's Vieux Carré. Owen built his restaurant into a famous institution overnight, competing with New Orleans' oldest and best in French and Creole cuisine. Owen's research and knowledge of French food, fine wine, and impeccable service made him a master. He was called the "wonder man" of the New Orleans restaurant industry. Owen's Irish stubbornness compelled him to work extremely long hours to put Brennan's on the culinary map—locally and nationwide.

Brennan's, as Owen ultimately wanted his restaurant to be called, became such a lucrative venture that when the time came to renew the lease on the Bourbon Street building, the landlord demanded fifty percent of the business. Unwilling to meet these demands, Owen moved the restaurant to its present location on Royal Street.

In 1954, Owen leased the building and began renovating and redecorating the Patio Royal at 417 Royal Street to convert it into the new Brennan's Restaurant. On November 1, 1955, Owen invited Brennan's initial customers to join him at his officially opened bar located in the building carriageway. The opening of the restaurant was scheduled for the spring

of 1956, but the hand of fate dealt a devastating blow.

Shortly before the grand opening, Owen Edward Brennan died of a massive coronary. Although shock and grief overwhelmed his family and the friends who loved him so dearly, Brennan's Restaurant still opened in its new Royal Street location on schedule.

In its new location on Royal Street, Brennan's prospered as it had on Bourbon Street. Owen's multitude of friends continued to patronize the restaurant he had founded, even though their good friend was no longer there. Owen's ingenious concept of "Breakfast at Brennan's" and the dishes that were invented under his scrutiny, including Bananas Foster and Eggs Hussarde, combined with the expertise of his Dutch Chef Paul Blangé, have made Brennan's world-famous.

OYSTERS ROCKEFELLER SOUP

Serves 8

2 cups (about 48) shucked oysters
2 quarts cold water
³/₄ cup (1 ¹/₂ sticks) butter
³/₄ cup celery, chopped
¹/₂ cup all-purpose flour
¹/₃ cup Pernod or Herbsaint (optional)
8 ounces fresh spinach leaves, washed, stemmed, and coarsely chopped
¹/₄ cup fresh parsley, finely chopped
Salt and white pepper to taste
2 cups heavy cream

Place the oysters in a large saucepan and cover with 2 quarts cold water. Cook over medium heat just until the oysters begin to curl, about 5 minutes.

Strain the oysters, reserving the stock. Set oysters aside.

Melt the butter in a large pot and sauté the celery until tender. Stir in the flour, and then add oysters and oyster stock. Reduce heat and simmer for 10 minutes until thickened.

Add the Pernod, spinach, and parsley; season to taste with salt and pepper. Pour in the cream and simmer several minutes until the soup is hot, and then serve.

> *"A gourmet is just a glutton with brains."*
> Philip W. Haberman

BANANAS FOSTER

Serves 4

$1/4$ cup butter

1 cup brown sugar

$1/2$ teaspoon cinnamon

$1/4$ cup banana liqueur

4 bananas, cut in half lengthwise, then halved

$1/4$ cup dark rum

4 scoops vanilla ice cream

Combine the butter, sugar, and cinnamon in a flambé pan or skillet. Place the pan over low heat either on an alcohol burner or on top of the stove and cook, stirring, until the sugar dissolves.

Stir in the banana liqueur, then place the bananas in the pan. When the banana sections soften and begin to brown, carefully add the rum. Continue to cook the sauce until the rum is hot, then tip the pan slightly to ignite the rum.

When the flames subside, lift the bananas out of the pan and place four pieces over each portion of ice cream.

Generously spoon warm sauce over the top of the ice cream and serve immediately.

Hotel Maison de Ville

Maison de Ville and

The Audubon Cottages

727 Rue Toulouse

New Orleans, Louisiana 70130

(504) 561-5858 or

(800) 634-1600

www.hotelmaisondeville.com

Like the city of New Orleans itself, the word "Creole" vibrates with a rich and complex history. It's a spicy amalgam of influences from the Old World and the New, a European and Afro-Caribbean fusion that is a testament to the rich melting pot of New Orleans' native culture.

Just what is a Creole? The answer to that question has morphed over the years, and even today there are as many as 30 definitions for the word. Originally, the term referred to the descendents of French and Spanish colonists who flocked to the city in the early eighteenth century. By the time of the Louisiana Purchase in 1803, the definition had expanded to include any native of New Orleans, including the large population of "gens de couleur libre," free persons of color as well as slaves born in the city.

After Louisiana became part of the United States, a growing number of white, English-speaking people moved to New Orleans and settled mainly in the uptown area. Meanwhile, the native Creoles dominated the city's downtown, including the French Quarter. As time wore on, white New Orleanians dissociated themselves from the term "Creole," and the word came to refer to the non-white population native to New Orleans. Today, it generally refers to anyone who can trace his or her roots back to the early inhabitants of the city.

Creole is not Cajun. Many mistakenly use the terms Creole and Cajun interchangeably, but they refer to two very distinct groups of people. Cajuns descended from French Canadians who immigrated to the rural areas of the Louisiana bayou. The cosmopolitan city of New Orleans is Creole territory. Growing interest in African-American history has focused more attention on the unique Creole culture of New Orleans.

Creole culture has had a long and profound impact on the city of New Orleans, bringing a heritage of delicious food, lively music, colorful dialect, and fascinating folklore. These elements of Creole culture are—like the people themselves—unique mixtures of influences from the Caribbean, Africa, Europe, and Native America.

The historic Maison de Ville property is comprised of a two-story town home and four slave quarters across the courtyard. It is believed that these are some of the city's oldest structures, dating back to the mid-1700s. Now renovated into sixteen luxuriously appointed guest rooms and suites, the chambers are furnished with four-poster beds, antiques, marble basins, paintings, and accessories. High ceilings, hardwood floors, and oriental rugs offer modern comfort in an old-world setting.

Room nine is known as the Tennessee Williams Room because it was the playwright's room of choice. Featuring a king-sized bed, the room is located on the ground floor and is accessed through the courtyard. Williams used the courtyard while writing *A Streetcar Named Desire*.

The Audubon Cottages, named after the naturalist and author John James Audubon, offer an additional seven accommodations. Audubon, worked on a number of his famed Birds of America series of paintings from cottage number one in 1921. Cottage one shares a courtyard with cottage seven, which originally served as a slave quarters.

Cottage two offers two bedrooms—one King Bedroom and one four-poster canopied double—with private baths, one of which has a Jacuzzi tub. The large hardwood-floored living room has plenty of seating and a dining room table, and the private courtyard offers seating for

four. Celebrities such as Elizabeth Taylor have stayed in this cottage (which is reputedly haunted!).

The pool at the Audubon Cottages is said to be the oldest in the French Quarter. Set in original brick, the pool is surrounded by lush foliage and offers seating in wrought iron chaise lounges.

Celebrities like Mick Jagger, Ed Bradley, Kevin Costner, Paul Newman and Joan Woodward, Jeremy Irons, and Dan Aykroyd have all taken advantage of the beauty of this unique hotel and its Bistro Restaurant.

CHOCOLATE CRÈME BRÛLÉE

Serves 8–10

6 egg yolks

³/₄ cup granulated sugar

1 quart heavy cream

6 ounces good quality (such as Callebaut) chocolate, finely and evenly chopped

1 vanilla bean, seeds scraped

Combine yolks and sugar in mixing bowl. Bring cream to simmer, add vanilla seeds and chocolate. Let rest in order for chocolate to melt. Add cooled cream mixture to sugar and yolk mixture and blend.

Place in ramekins, in bain-marie, in 350-degree oven for approximately 20 minutes, until set. Remove and chill. Use salamander or propane torch to caramelize sugar on top of cooled brûlée. Serve.

> *"There are only three great storybook cities in America—*
> *New York, San Francisco and New Orleans."*
> Tennessee Williams

CELERIAC REMOULADE WITH BELGIAN ENDIVE AND PEPPERED SMOKED MACKEREL

Serves 4

1 medium bulb celeriac (celery root) peeled, shredded with mandolin (or julienned), blanched and shocked with ice water, drained dry

1 small red onion, minced

1 tablespoon capers

$\frac{1}{8}$ teaspoon cayenne pepper

1 tablespoon Worcestershire sauce

1 tablespoon prepared Creole mustard

1 teaspoon tomato ketchup

1 cup (preferably homemade) mayonnaise

Juice of one lemon

2 heads Belgian endive, washed and trimmed

$\frac{3}{4}$ pound smoked mackerel fillets, flaked and deboned

Combine cayenne, salt, pepper, Worcestershire, mustard, and ketchup into mayonnaise. Pour mixture over prepared celeriac. Add lemon juice, capers, and red onion. (Prepare ahead of time—remoulade sauce gets better in refrigerator overnight.)

Arrange remoulade in center of plate. Place endive around remoulade. Top with smoked mackerel (high-quality peppered, smoked fish available in fine delis or grocery stores.)

Acme Oyster House

Acme Oyster House has been pleasing the palates of discriminating diners since 1910. Originally located around the corner at 117 Royal Street, the Acme Café, as it was then called, was nestled next to the old Cosmopolitan Hotel, described by the *New Orleans Item* as "the scene of the making and breaking of Louisiana politicians ..."

In 1924, a disastrous fire caused the collapse of the three-story Acme Saloon building. The Café was then reestablished as the Acme Oyster House at its present location in the French Quarter.

One year after the structure at 724 Iberville was constructed, the town of Covington, Louisiana, was founded. In 1997, after nearly ninety years of operation, Acme Oyster House chose Covington's Downtown Historic District for its first new establishment. Another location was opened in 1998 on Lakeshore Drive in New Orleans' famous West End Lakefront District. It occupies the space beneath Aqua's The Pearl nightclub.

Acme's legendary status as a New Orleans classic has caused the Oyster House to be featured on several national TV programs, including *The Mark Russell Special,* broadcast from New Orleans in October 2000. Acme is defined as "the highest point or stage." The Oyster House staff works hard to be the "acme of cold saltiness."

Acme Oyster House

724 Iberville Street

New Orleans, Louisiana 70130

(504)522-5973

"He is a very valiant man who first ventured on eating of oysters."
Thomas Fuller

OYSTERS LOUISIANA

Serves 6

4 ounces (1 stick) butter, melted

1 1/2 pints oysters, drained

4 green onions, finely chopped

3 cloves garlic, minced

1/2 pound fresh lump crabmeat

1/2 cup bread crumbs

Salt and pepper to taste

Melt butter in a skillet. Add oysters and cook until dry. Add onions and garlic and cook slowly for at least 10 minutes.

Fold in crabmeat and crumbs. Simmer 5 minutes more. Add salt and pepper to taste.

Broussard's

Broussard's

819 Rue Conti

New Orleans, Louisiana 70112

(504) 581-3866

www.broussards.com

A local institution for nearly 80 years, Broussard's embodies the legend, glamour, and history of New Orleans. In 1920, Joseph Broussard, a Frenchman of fiery temperament, and his wife, Rosalie Borrello, opened a restaurant in the nineteenth-century French Quarter townhouse that had been Rosalie's home. (It was built in 1824 at a then-extravagant cost of $700.00; the rear dining room is in what was once the stables.) Thus, the legend was born.

Joseph Broussard created classic French dishes inspired by his formal Parisian culinary training. His traditional yet innovative style of cooking attracted both locals and visitors. Broussaud's became a favorite dining spot for writers living in New Orleans (William Faulkner and Tennessee Williams among them) and film stars visiting the Crescent City (Spencer Tracy, Clark Gable, and Marilyn Monroe were just a few.)

Papa Joe was an eccentric. He greatly admired Napoleon Bonaparte and, as a tribute to his hero, had a statue of the Emperor erected in the restaurant's courtyard. Every time a guest ordered a napoleon brandy, the waiters would gather around the statue and, under the direction of Papa Joe himself, launch into a spirited rendition of "La Marseillaise." Broussard was a true original, one of a trio of noted New Orleans restaurateurs that also included Antoine Alciatore and Count Arnaud Cazenave.

Broussard could have left his legacy in no better hands than those of Gunter Preuss. Chef Preuss has, for the past 35 years, built a reputation among American and international food critics as New Orleans' premier interpreter of classic Creole cuisine. Profiled in the PBS series *Great Chefs of New Orleans* and a recent recipient of the Millennium Chef International Award of Excellence, Gunter—along with wife Evelyn and son Marc—has brought excitement back to 819 Conti Street. This excitement comes not only from the elegance and style of the restaurant, but also from such signature dishes as Louisiana Bouillabaisse, Veal Acadian and Pompano Napoleon, as well as delectable desserts such as Crêpes Broussard.

The excellence of Chef Preuss' cuisine is complemented by the restaurant's

Sweet Potato, Shrimp, and Corn Bisque

Serves 18–20

3 tablespoons butter

1 medium yellow onion, diced

1 tablespoon dried thyme

1 tablespoon paprika

1 gallon shrimp stock (use water from shrimp)

16 ounces frozen corn

$\frac{1}{2}$ quart heavy cream

1 pound sweet potato, grated

2 cups instant mashed potato

2 pounds 36/42 shrimp, cooked and peeled

In heavy pot, melt butter and sauté onion and thyme. Add paprika, stock, corn, and heavy cream. Bring to a boil. Reduce heat and simmer 15 minutes. Add sweet potato and mashed potato, and simmer another 5 minutes. Add shrimp and serve.

three elegant dining rooms, each with its own distinctive personality. The small, private dining rooms overlook a lush courtyard that *New Orleans* magazine calls "the most beautiful in the French Quarter." When weather permits, the courtyard makes an ideal spot for dining, while Broussard's charming piano bar is the perfect place for a before- or after-dinner cocktail.

There are few restaurants in the city that can match the classic ambiance of this historic landmark.

BROUSSARD'S BOUILLABAISSE

Serves 6

Broth

$^1\!/_2$ pound carrots, chopped

$^1\!/_2$ cup tomato paste

$^1\!/_2$ pound celery ribs, chopped

1 gallon shrimp or fish stock

$^1\!/_2$ pound onions, chopped

2 cups tomatoes, chopped

$^1\!/_2$ fennel bulb

6 strands ($^1\!/_8$ ounce) saffron

$^1\!/_2$ green pepper, seeded and chopped

Salt to taste

$^1\!/_2$ cup olive oil

White pepper to taste

1 tablespoon chopped garlic

3 bay leaves

$^1\!/_4$ cup chopped shallots

Peel and split the carrots and slice them diagonally. Slice the celery the same way. Cut the onions, fennel, and green peppers in a similar fashion.

In a suitable stockpot, heat the olive oil. Sauté the carrots, celery, and fennel until half-cooked. Add the onions, peppers, garlic, and shallots. When the mixture is thoroughly heated, stir in the tomato paste and cook for 10 minutes, stirring regularly. Then add the stock, preferably lukewarm. Add the tomatoes, crushing and draining by hand as you go. Then add the saffron, already "steeped" in hot water, salt and pepper, and bay leaves. Bring to a full boil.

Remove from heat, cool, and chill.

Bouillabaisse Seafood

1 pound raw shrimp, peeled and de-veined

$^1\!/_2$ pound fresh fish fillets, trout, pompano etc., cut into 1-inch cubes

1 cup raw oysters

$^1\!/_2$ pound lump crabmeat

$^1\!/_2$ pound raw scallops

$^1\!/_2$ pound crawfish tail meat, peeled

18 fresh mussels

When ready to complete and serve the bouillabaisse, heat the broth in a soup pot to a boil. Add the shrimp, oysters, crabmeat, crawfish, fish, scallops, and mussels. Bring back to a simmer and cook for about 5 minutes, or just enough time for the seafood to be cooked but not overdone. Serve.

CRABMEAT BROUSSARD

Serves 6

1 tablespoon butter

6 jumbo shrimp, peeled, tail left on,
   de-veined; butterfly

2 tablespoons olive oil

1 small yellow onion, diced

2 fresh artichoke hearts, chopped

1 large clove garlic, minced

$^1/_4$ cup flour

$^1/_4$ cup white wine

2 cups chicken stock

1 cup heavy cream

3 ounces brie cheese

$^1/_2$ cup bread crumbs

3 tablespoons olive oil

1 tablespoon whole fresh thyme leaves

$^3/_4$ pound jumbo lump crabmeat

Preheat the oven to 400 degrees.

In a large skillet, melt the butter and sauté the shrimp until just cooked. Set aside to cool.

In a heavy saucepan, heat the olive oil and sauté the yellow onion, artichoke hearts, and garlic over medium heat until the onion becomes limp. Sprinkle in the flour and mix well, cooking for a minute more. Deglaze the pan with the white wine, then add stock. Bring to a boil, reduce heat, and simmer for three minutes. Add the heavy cream and simmer for another five minutes.

Take the brie and scrape off and discard the white skin; cut cheese into small pieces. Add brie to the cream sauce and stir until all of the cheese is melted and mixed well. Remove from heat and allow to cool.

In a small bowl, combine the bread crumbs, olive oil, and thyme. Set aside.

After the cheese mixture is cool, gently fold in the crabmeat, being careful not break up the lumps.

To assemble, place one shrimp standing up in the center of an oven-proof serving dish. Spoon the crabmeat mixture around the shrimp and sprinkle with the bread crumb mixture. Repeat with the remaining shrimp. Arrange the dishes on a large baking pan and bake in the preheated oven for fifteen minutes, or until the crab mixture is hot and bubbly. Serve immediately.

This dish was served to Steven Segal on a "film" visit to New Orleans.

49

Jimmy Buffett's Margaritaville

Stepping into Jimmy Buffett's Margaritaville in New Orleans is like stepping back in time. The structure was originally used as both a slave quarters and a slave-auction building. After abolition of slavery, the building served a variety of functions. One report has it housing a noodle factory for a period of time.

The French Market side of the property was a produce warehouse for most of its existence. The Decatur side is a series of four town homes with commercial first floors. Part of the Decatur Street side was Palace Pride 24-hour burger joint back in the '50s—which is why the neon sign looks like a palace. The neon sign is one of only two such signs in existence in the area. The Vieux Carré Commission (the group that exists to protect the history of the French Quarter) will not let management take it down or swap it out with another. The second-oldest sign is in front of Tujague's.

Following the burger years, the building was Storyville Tavern, a music venue that lasted until Margaritaville was opened in 1953. The tavern had some big-name acts play on its stage. Some believe that Storyville might have been named after the red light district nearby, but it had nothing to do with that area of town. Storyville was originally located right outside of the French Quarter, but it is no longer there. It has been replaced by a Winn Dixie and some housing projects.

The existing balcony, properly called a gallery, was added in 2002. It reflects a smaller set of basket galleries that burned in a fire around 1900.

Jimmy Buffett's Margaritaville

1104 Decatur

New Orleans, Louisiana 70116

(504) 592-2565

www.margaritaville.com

CRAWFISH DIP

Yields 4 cups

8 ounces chopped crawfish tails

$^3/_4$ cup yellow onion, chopped

$^3/_4$ cup green bell peppers, chopped

$^3/_4$ cup celery, chopped

$^3/_4$ cup poblano peppers, chopped

$^3/_4$ cup red bell peppers, chopped

1 tablespoon shrimp base

1 teaspoon basil

1 teaspoon thyme

1 teaspoon white pepper

1 teaspoon black pepper

1 teaspoon kosher salt

1 pound cream cheese

4 ounces sherry

$^1/_2$ cup heavy cream

1 tablespoon Matouks Flambeau Sauce

In a steam kettle, sauté crawfish and vegetables until onions become translucent. Add shrimp base and all spices and cook for 5 minutes.

Add cream cheese and sherry. Reduce for 10 minutes. Add Matouks and heavy cream. Stir until well incorporated.

Serve with Garlic French toast points.

ROSARITA MARGARITA

Serves 1

1 ½ ounces Margaritaville Gold Tequila

½ ounce Cointreau

3 ounces Sour Mix

1 ounce Cranberry Juice

12-ounce Gibraltar glass

Lemon wedge

Tall straw

Sugar for glass rim

Build in mixing tin. Shake without ice.

Wet rim of Gibraltar glass with lemon wedge and dip in sugar to "frost" the lip of the glass.

Pour mixture over ice into Gibraltar glass. Add a tall straw and lemon wedge.

MARGARITAVILLE MOJITO

Serves 1

¼ cup fresh mint leaves

½ ounce fresh lime juice

2 ounces Mount Gay Sugar Cane Rum

2 ½ ounces simple syrup

2 ¾ ounces soda water

16-ounce (1 pint) glass

Lime slices

Tall straw

Muddle mint and lime juice in pint glass. Fill pint glass with ice. Add rum and simple syrup. Shake vigorously.

Top with soda water. Add tall straw and lime slice for garnish.

"We may live without friends, we may live without books,
but civilized man cannot live without cooks.
He may live without love—what is passion but pining?
But where is the man who can live without dining?"
Bulwer Lytton

GUMBO

Serves 8–10

4 tablespoons (2 ounces) butter

6 tablespoons flour

$\frac{1}{2}$ pound Andouille sausage, sliced into $\frac{1}{4}$-inch
   half moons

$\frac{1}{2}$ pound cooked chicken thigh meat, deboned

$\frac{1}{2}$ cup yellow onions, chopped

$\frac{1}{4}$ cup green bell peppers, chopped

$\frac{1}{4}$ cup celery, chopped

1 tablespoon garlic, minced

1 tablespoon shrimp base

1 $\frac{1}{2}$ quarts water

$\frac{1}{2}$ teaspoon Tabasco

1 $\frac{1}{2}$ tablespoons Worcestershire sauce

$\frac{1}{2}$ teaspoon salt

1 $\frac{1}{2}$ teaspoons crushed red pepper
   (adjust as needed for desired taste)

1 $\frac{1}{2}$ cups frozen okra, cooked

$\frac{3}{4}$ pound 36/40 count shrimp, peeled and
   deveined

$\frac{1}{4}$ cup crab claw meat (picked)

Heat the butter in a saucepan and add the flour. Simmer over medium heat and cook, stirring constantly until the roux is cooked and light brown.

Chop chicken into $\frac{1}{2}$-inch pieces and sauté with the sausage in another saucepot for 5 minutes.

Add vegetables and garlic and sauté till limp. Add roux, salt, and red pepper and mix well. Add water and incorporate with roux. Bring to a simmer.

Add shrimp base, Tabasco, and Worcestershire and simmer for 30 minutes.

Add okra, shrimp, and crab. Cook 30 additional minutes.

Serve with white rice and French bread.

53

Muriel's

Muriel's

801 Chartres Street

New Orleans, Louisiana 70116

(504) 568-1885

www.muriels.com

In 1718, the year New Orleans was founded, a young French Canadian named Claude Trepagnier was a member of the expedition party led by Bienville that carved a clearing on the bank of the river and named it Ville de la Nouvelle Orleans. As a reward for his participation in the expedition, Claude Trepagnier was granted a plot of land where he constructed a brick house with a bark-shingled roof, a brick chimney, and a front gallery.

When the official design of the city was constructed in 1721, the grid pattern of the streets was laid out, with the center being the Place de Armes (parade grounds), which is now Jackson Square. The central focus of the traditionally-designed French town was the cathedral. Claude Trepagnier's house became a key plot of land during this time.

Sometime between 1743 and 1762, Jean Baptiste Destrehan, the Royal Treasurer of the French Louisiana Colonies, acquired Trepagnier's property. A man of great wealth and power in New Orleans, he tore down the humble cottage and built a suitably fine home for his family. His residence was second only to the French Colonial Governor's Mansion, which stood where the Presbytere is today. He outfitted and furnished the house with the best linens, fabrics, drapes, rugs, furniture, china, crystal, and silver, all of which was imported from Paris.

After the death of Destrehan in 1765, the house passed to his son and was then sold at auction when the family money ran out. In 1776, Pierre Phillipe de Marigny purchased the grand residence. Marigny used the house as one of his "city homes" when he came into town from his plantation on the outskirts of town (now the Fauberg Marigny).

In 1788, a major fire swept through the French Quarter. The elegant residence was partially burned. Marigny sold the property to Pierre Jourdan, who rebuilt the house using the remaining portions of the buildings that were still standing. During renovation of Muriel's, many of the original charred walls and beams were uncovered.

From 1823 to 1861, the house was owned by Julien Poydras, President of the Louisiana State Senate and a director of the Louisiana Bank. Poydras Street is named after Julien Poydras. He purchased the residence and refurnished it with lavish fineries. A year after moving into the home, he became ill and died. His widow and family continued to live in the home throughout New Orleans' heyday. They used the home as a place to entertain while away from their six plantations.

During the Civil War and for several years after, the Poydras family continued to own the home. In 1881, they sold it to Theodore Leveau, who owned the property for ten years. During the years after the Civil War, hard times fell on the once-rich city. Wealthy plantation owners such as the Poydras family were hit hardest. Much of the wealth and power had shifted from the old French families of the French Quarter to the American sector in the Garden District and Uptown. The houses and properties in the French Quarter began to fall into decay and were considered unfashionable.

Peter Lipari, who had made a fortune in cornering the orange market, purchased the building and remodeled the façade to its present look. The building was converted to a series of commercial businesses—Hill's restaurant used a portion it, and the Jackson Square corner was converted into a bar, The Alec Lanlois Saloon, by 1895. The saloon was the

home of the well-known "Royal Club," a drinking club of notable New Orleanians, "organized for fun, pure and simple."

In 1916, Frank Taormina purchased the building and turned it into a pasta factory and first-floor grocery store. The building was then converted into a restaurant called The Spaghetti Factory. Muriel's Jackson Square opened its doors on March 10, 2001, after an extensive restoration of the building to its former mid-1800s glory.

CRAWFISH CRÊPES

Yields 12 filled crêpes
Crawfish Filling
1 tablespoon oil
2 tablespoons yellow onion, diced
1 tablespoon bell pepper, diced
2 tablespoons tomato, diced
$^1/_4$ teaspoon garlic, chopped
1 teaspoon Creole seasoning
$^1/_2$ cup crawfish tails
2 tablespoons unsalted butter
Salt and pepper

Crêpes Topping
$^1/_4$ cup plus 2 tablespoons goat cheese
$^1/_4$ cup cream cheese
$^1/_2$ teaspoon shallot, chopped
$^1/_2$ teaspoon chives, chopped

$^1/_4$ teaspoon salt
$^1/_4$ teaspoon pepper

Prepare 12 crepes (see recipe, page 30). Place oil in sauté pan over medium high heat. Add onions and peppers and sauté until softened.

Add tomato, garlic, and Creole seasoning and sauté for 30 seconds. Add crawfish, sauté 30 seconds more, then add white wine.

Reduce slightly, then add butter. Adjust seasoning with salt and pepper and fill the crêpes.

For the crêpes topping: mix all ingredients together and pour over warm, filled crêpes.

EGGPLANT AND SHRIMP STUFFING

Yields 24 filled crêpes
1 pound eggplant, peeled and diced
$^1/_4$ cup plus 2 tablespoons bell pepper, diced
$^1/_4$ cup celery, diced
$^1/_2$ cup onion, diced
$^1/_2$ cup tomato, diced
$1^1/_2$ teaspoons fresh basil, chiffonade
$^3/_4$ pound raw shrimp, peeled
1 cup French bread, diced
$^1/_2$ cup seafood stock
$1^1/_2$ teaspoons chopped garlic
$1^1/_2$ teaspoons parmesan cheese

Prepare 24 crêpes (see recipe, page 30). Sauté onions, peppers, and celery until softened. Add eggplant, garlic and tomato, and sauté one minute.

Add shrimp and basil. Cook until shrimp are almost done.

Add seafood stock and French bread. Add parmesan cheese and season with salt and pepper.

Cook at 375 degrees for 20 minutes.

MURIEL'S BARBECUE SHRIMP

Serves 2

Spicy Butter Sauce

1 ¹/₂ cups Abita Amber (beer)

³/₄ cup Worcestershire Sauce

1 tablespoon shallot, finely chopped

¹/₂ tablespoon garlic, finely chopped

¹/₂ cup heavy cream

1 tablespoon Creole seasoning

1 ¹/₄ tablespoons cracked black pepper

1 tablespoon lemon juice

1 tablespoon rosemary, chopped

4 cups unsalted butter, cubed

¹/₄ teaspoon fish sauce

Barbecue Shrimp

8 10/15 shrimp, shelled, de-veined and grilled

¹/₂ cup cooked rice

¹/₂ cup Spicy Butter Sauce

Place beer, Worcestershire, and shallot in a pot and reduce until almost all liquid is evaporated. Add cream and reduce until thickened.

Lower heat to low and start whisking in butter. When all butter is incorporated, remove from heat. Whisk in remaining ingredients.

Gumbo Shop

Gumbo Shop

630 Saint Peter Street

(504) 525-1486

New Orleans, Louisiana 70130

(800) 55GUMBO

www.gumboshop.com

New Orleans was founded by the French in 1718 and named after the regent, the Duke d'Orleans. Passed to the Spanish for a while, it went back to France long enough for Napoleon to sell it to a fledgling United States of America in 1803.

In New Orleans, the French influence was just the beginning. Through the years, African slaves were often cooks. Through this busy port have come new citizens from Germany, Ireland, the French Caribbean Islands, Italy, Greece, Croatia, and, more recently, Asia.

The Choctaw Indians were already living in this swampy, mosquito-infested piece of land that sits below sea level on the Mississippi River. They introduced powdered sassafras—or filé—to settlers as a staple of the indigenous soup we call gumbo. A gumbo usually contains either filé or okra as a thickener. Just as New Orleans is a blend of many cultures, so gumbo can be made with any blend of ingredients. However, the base of most gumbos is "roux"—flour and fat, browned to provide a nutty flavor.

The terms "Creole" and "Cajun" define New Orleans cooking. A word whose meaning has been transformed over the years, "Creole" generally refers to anything native to New Orleans. Traditionally it described a person of French and Spanish roots born in the colonies. Recently it has come to include African in the mix. When describing food, it refers to more sophisticated city cooking typical of New Orleans.

"Cajun" describes cooking from Southwest Louisiana, influenced by the legacy of the Acadians, descendants of French Canadian communities in Nova Scotia and New Brunswick who were expelled by the British in the middle 1700s. Cajun cooking is typically rich, hearty, and spicy. With other ethnic influences playing a part in both types of cooking, the line separating these two culinary styles has become as fuzzy as the outer skin of the green spindly okra.

The Gumbo Shop is located in one of America's most historic neighborhoods: the "Vieux Carré" (French for "old square"), also known as the French Quarter. Open since the 1920s as a restaurant, according to veteran New Orleans architect Henry Krotzer, this

Louisiana Colonial townhouse is one of a handful of eighteenth-century buildings left in the Quarter.

The structure was built in 1795 to replace a building that was destroyed in the devastating 1794 fire that started around the corner from the restaurant and almost wiped out the city. There was a commercial establishment downstairs and a residence above, typical of land use at that time. Among its more illustrious inhabitants was John Watkins, mayor of New Orleans in the early 1800s. The ground floor of the 200-year-old building was once a woodworking shop. The carriageway entry to the Gumbo Shop leads you either to an inviting tropical courtyard under a canopy of banana trees or a quaint interior lined with murals in warm gold-brown tones depicting scenes from New Orleans' past. Painted on the burlap wrappings of cotton bales in 1925 by local artist Marc Antony, the scenes are of the restaurant's neighbors, the Presbytere and the Cabildo—the earliest seats of government and the site of the Louisiana Purchase, respectively.

Above the ground floor of the Gumbo Shop building you might expect to find Stanley Kowalksi and his spouse, Stella. Tennessee Williams, who considered New Orleans his spiritual home, completed his Pulitzer Prize winning play *A Streetcar Named Desire* while living in an apartment on the top floor of the building next door at 632 Saint Peter. From the window of his apartment he could see "that rattletrap old streetcar" named Desire whose route included nearby Royal Street and Bourbon Street. Just a half block away towards the Mississippi River is Jackson Square, named for Andrew Jackson, the hero of the Battle of New Orleans who later became President of the United States. With the St. Louis Cathedral right in the center of the Square, "those Cathedral bells" that the tragic Blanche duBois referred to in *Streetcar* can be heard in the restaurant's courtyard. The Gumbo Shop is at ground zero when it comes to a quintessential New Orleans experience.

SEAFOOD OKRA GUMBO

Yields 6 entrees or 10–12 appetizers

2 pounds fresh or frozen shrimp, head on
   (about 40–50 count per pound)

2 small blue crabs, fresh or frozen

3 quarts water

2 tablespoons cooking oil

1 quart fresh or frozen okra, sliced into
   $^{1}/_{4}$-inch rounds

$^{2}/_{3}$ cup cooking oil

$^{1}/_{2}$ cup all-purpose flour

2 cups onion, chopped

1 cup green bell pepper, chopped

$^{1}/_{2}$ cup celery, chopped

1 teaspoon garlic, finely chopped

1 16-ounce can chopped tomatoes

2 bay leaves

2 teaspoons salt (or to taste)

$^{1}/_{2}$ teaspoon black pepper (or to taste)

$^{1}/_{2}$ teaspoon white pepper (or to taste)

$^{1}/_{4}$ teaspoon cayenne pepper (or to taste)

Peel and de-vein the shrimp refrigerate, covered. Rinse the shrimp shells and heads and place in a non-reactive stock pot along with 2 quarts of water. Bring to a boil, reduce heat, and simmer for 30–45 minutes to make a stock. Strain, discard the shells and heads and set the stock aside.

Meanwhile, wash the crabs well under running water, place in a non-reactive pot with 1 quart of water, bring to a boil, and simmer for 20–30 minutes. Strain, reserving stock and crabs. When the crabs are cool enough to handle, snap both claws off then break the body in half. Set aside.

In a heavy-bottomed skillet, heat 2 tablespoons of oil, add the okra and sauté over medium-high heat for about 10–15 minutes or until all the "ropiness" is gone. (This step may take a little longer if fresh okra is used. Frozen vegetables are usually plunged into boiling water and blanched before freezing, so they are partially cooked.)

Place the $^{2}/_{3}$ cup oil in a large (8-quart) heavy-bottomed non-reactive Dutch oven-type pot. Add the flour and, over a medium-high fire, make a dark brown roux. As soon as the proper color is achieved, add the onions, bell pepper, celery, and garlic and sauté, stirring occasionally until tender. During this process, allow the vegetables to stick to the bottom of the pan a bit, then scrape the bottom with a metal spoon or spatula. This allows some of the natural sugars in the onions to caramelize, rendering great depth of flavor.

When the seasoning vegetables are tender, add the tomatoes, bay leaves, the

Continued next page

three peppers, and a little salt. Cook for about 10 minutes, repeating the stick-and-scrape process with the tomatoes. Add the sautéed okra and cook for 10 more minutes. Add the crab stock and half of the shrimp stock to the pot. Stirring constantly, bring the pot to a boil. Lower the heat a bit, partially cover, and simmer for 30 minutes, stirring occasionally. If the gumbo appears too thick, add more stock to adjust. Add salt to taste and adjust the pepper if desired.

Add the broken crabs and simmer for about 10 minutes. Add the peeled shrimp, return to a boil, and simmer until the shrimp are firm and pink, about 5 minutes. Remove the pot from heat.

As is the case with most gumbos, this dish is best prepared either early on the day it is to be served, or even the day before, thereby allowing time for the flavors to marry. When reheating, stir often and be careful to avoid overcooking the shrimp.

Serve in large bowls over steamed rice.

SHRIMP AND SMOKED TOMATO MARINARA

Serves 8

2 pounds diced tomatoes, divided
$1/3$ cup extra-virgin olive oil
$2/3$ cup chopped onions
$1/4$ pound small mushrooms, quartered
1 tablespoon garlic, minced
2 teaspoon salt
1 teaspoon black pepper
1 teaspoon dried oregano
1 tablespoon fresh basil, chopped
1 pound peeled raw shrimp, medium size
$3/4$ pound dried pasta, such as penne or rotini

Spread 1 pound of the diced tomatoes on a small roasting pan and smoke for 20 minutes in a backyard smoker or covered barbecue grill according to the manufacturer's directions. Set aside.

In a large saucepan set over medium heat, sauté the chopped onion in the olive oil until tender. Add the mushrooms, garlic, salt, pepper, and oregano and cook for 1 minute. Add the smoked tomatoes and the other pound of diced tomatoes and bring pot to a boil. Reduce heat and simmer for 5 minutes. Add the shrimp and cook for about 5 minutes, or until shrimp are just done. Stir in the basil and turn off heat.

Meanwhile, cook the pasta according to the package directions. Drain well and toss with sauce in a large preheated bowl. Serve immediately.

Dickie Brennan's Steakhouse

Dickie Brennan's Steakhouse

716 Iberville Street

New Orleans, Louisiana 70130

(504) 522-CHOP

www.dbrennanssteakhouse.com

Having grown up a member of the famed New Orleans restaurant family, Dickie Brennan has always known the restaurant business as a way of life. Dickie entered the restaurant business in 1974, gaining his first culinary experience at his family's restaurant Commander's Palace, under the tutelage of world-renowned chef Paul Prudhomme.

Dickie was a part of the opening team of the family's next venture, Mr. B's Bistro, which has now been in operation for more than twenty years. While receiving extensive training at Commander's Palace and Mr. B's Bistro, he attended LSU and Loyola, earning a degree in finance. During his college years, Dickie spent a semester studying in Rome, Italy, and served an apprenticeship at Delmonico's restaurant in Mexico City, Mexico.

Upon graduation, at a time when American food was on the cutting edge of the culinary world, Dickie left for New York to apprentice with famed chef Larry Forgione of An American Place restaurant. He then moved to France to study the French language at the Institute de Française and to cook in some of Paris' most famous restaurants: La Tour d' Argent, Taillevent, Chilberta, Au Quai d' Orsay, La Maree, and Gerard Besson.

Dickie returned to the United States in 1985 to be General Manager of the family's restaurant, Brennan's of Houston, in downtown Houston, Texas. Four years later, Dickie moved home to New Orleans to convert the historic, turn-of-the-century Werlein building into a grand café, much like the ones he had known in Paris. On March 11, 1991, Palace Café was born, with Dickie functioning as Managing Partner for the family.

After the first year of Palace Café's operation, Dickie's role expanded to include the duties of Executive Chef. To date, Dickie is the only family member to have held this position. In 1995, sixteen years after his departure, Dickie returned to Commander's Palace as Managing Partner and assumed the day-to-day responsibilities of managing the restaurant from his father and his father's siblings.

With the senior generation's two goals of easing into retirement and finalizing the family's business succession plans accomplished, Dickie's dream of owning

and operating his own restaurant company became a reality. Dickie returned to Palace Café as Owner/ Managing Partner in November 1997. Committed to and inspired by his vision of creating a restaurant group focused on quality, value, continuous improvement, creativity, hospitality, and passion for excellence, he established Dickie Brennan & Company, which provides management services for Palace Café, Dickie Brennan's Steakhouse, and the group's newest restaurant, Bourbon House, which opened in October 2002 on world-famous Bourbon Street. Dickie and his father Dick Brennan are also partners in Mr. B's Bistro.

Dickie Brennan's Steakhouse was born on November 21, 1998. Soon after opening, it was recognized as one of the top steakhouses in America. With plans to expand and diversify his restaurant group, Dickie is committed to excellence in fine dining.

Located on Iberville, between Bourbon and Royal Streets, in the historic New Orleans French Quarter, Dickie Brennan's Steakhouse is tucked into a former parking garage that has been transformed into an inviting and cozy restaurant.

BARBECUE RIB-EYE

Serves 4

4 14-ounce rib-eyes

12 large head-on shrimp

2 bunches asparagus

2 tablespoons olive oil
(to rub asparagus before grilling)

Creole seasoning (to rub on steaks and
asparagus before grilling)

New Orleans Barbecue Sauce

1 tablespoon butter

1 teaspoon garlic, chopped

2 teaspoons cracked black pepper

2 teaspoons Creole seasoning

3 tablespoons Worcestershire sauce

1 tablespoon hot pepper sauce
(we use Crystal hot sauce)

Juice of 1 lemon

1 cup Amber beer
(we use a local brew, Abita Amber)

1/2 pound cold butter, diced

1 teaspoon fresh rosemary, minced

Season steaks and asparagus and grill over an open flame until asparagus are tender and steaks are cooked to temperature.

Melt butter in a medium-sized sauté pan and lightly toast garlic. Add the shrimp and cook for one minute on each side.

Increase the heat to high and add pepper, Creole seasoning, Worcestershire sauce, hot sauce, and lemon juice. Stir well, then deglaze with beer and reduce by half.

Lower heat to medium and add cold butter one piece at a time, stirring constantly and adding additional butter only after all previously added butter has been incorporated into the sauce. Sauce will thicken and should coat your spoon. Stir in fresh rosemary.

Lay asparagus on plate and place steak over asparagus (angled on the bias). Place shrimp on the side of steak and pour New Orleans Barbecue Sauce over shrimp and steak.

A prime 14-ounce rib-eye served with grilled asparagus and finished with New Orleans Barbecue Shrimp.

BANANAS FOSTER BREAD PUDDING

Serves 12–16

4 12-inch loaves French bread,
1 quart heavy cream
1 ¹/₂ cups whole milk
1 ¹/₂ cups sugar
3 cups light brown sugar
12 egg yolks
3 bananas
1 cup rum
¹/₂ teaspoon ground cinnamon
4 tablespoons vanilla extract
Vanilla ice cream
Fresh mint for garnish

Slice French bread and dry in a 200-degree oven for 20 minutes.

Combine remaining pudding ingredients and blend well with a hand mixer.

Thinly slice dried French bread and place in an 8- by 10- by 2-inch pan. Pour pudding into pan and mush all bread by hand so that the liquid is absorbed and the bread becomes very soggy. Be sure to flatten all of the lumps.

Cover pan with foil and bake at 300 degrees for 2½ hours, or until a skewer inserted in the center of the pudding comes out dry. Remove foil and bake for an additional 20 minutes, or until golden brown. Set aside to cool.

Rum Raisin Crème Anglaise

¹/₂ quart heavy cream
1 ¹/₂ cups sugar
10 egg yolks
1 cup rum
1 cup dark raisins

Bring heavy cream and sugar to a boil in a large, heavy saucepot.

Place egg yolks in a mixing bowl and slowly pour in hot cream and sugar, stirring vigorously with a wooden spoon to temper the yolks, being careful not to scramble them.

Once yolks have been tempered, return mixture to stove. Reduce heat to low, and stir constantly until sauce thickens enough to coat the back of your spoon.

Strain through a fine strainer into a large container and refrigerate until crème anglaise has fully cooled.

Cook rum and raisins over medium heat until alcohol has evaporated. Watch out for the flame! Refrigerate until fully cooled. Stir rum and raisins into crème anglaise. You may add more rum or omit it from the recipe, depending on taste.

To serve, cut bread pudding into 3½-inch squares. Top with vanilla ice cream, ladle with rum raisin crème anglaise, and garnish with mint leaves.

BACCO

BACCO

310 Chartres

New Orleans, Louisiana 70130

(504) 539-5522

In 1991, Ralph Brennan and his sister opened BACCO, a New Orleans Italian restaurant located in the French Quarter just around the block from Mr. B's. Consistently awarded "4 bean" ratings by the *Times-Picayune* and "4 star" ratings by *Menu* magazine's Tom Fitzmorris, BACCO was also selected as one of America's "Best New Restaurants of 1992" by John Mariani for *Esquire* magazine. BACCO consistently has been named "New Orleans' Best Italian Restaurant" by local publications, and The 2004 *Zagat* Survey notes BACCO as one of New Orleans' "Most Popular," "Best Italian," and "Most Romantic" restaurants.

Ralph Brennan entered the family business in the early 1980s after a successful stint as a Certified Public Accountant with Price, Waterhouse & Company. One of eight third-generation cousins actively involved in the restaurant industry today, Ralph Brennan and his cousins run twelve New Orleans-style restaurants, nine of which are located in New Orleans.

Ralph Brennan is the owner and operator of Red Fish Grill and BACCO in the New Orleans French Quarter, Ralph's on the Park in Mid-City New Orleans, and the Jazz Kitchen, located in the Downtown Disney® District at the Disneyland® Resort. Ralph is a co-owner of Mr. B's Bistro, Commander's Palace, and Brennan's of Houston.

Ralph Brennan's family entered the hospitality business in 1947 with the purchase of the Old Absinthe Bar on Bourbon Street in the New Orleans French Quarter. The family eventually left that business to operate a small restaurant, Brennan's Vieux Carré that eventually would become Brennan's on Royal Street. In 1969, Ralph Brennan's family purchased Commander's Palace in the historic New Orleans Garden District. Built in 1883, Commander's Palace has a long and colorful history.

In 1979, the Commander's Palace Brennans opened Mr. B's Bistro on Royal Street in the French Quarter. The location they chose was the old Solari's Delicatessen. Like that of its predecessors, the site for Mr. B's was in part chosen for its historical value. To this day, Ralph Brennan and his family pride themselves on the

tradition of the appreciation for and enhancement of each new location's individual and historical significance.

Known for redefining Italian cuisine in New Orleans, BACCO has won over many a guest with its stunning array of local and regional ingredients prepared using traditional Italian cooking methods. The results of the marriage of Creole and Italian cooking are nothing short of spectacular.

BLACK TRUFFLE FETTUCCINE

Serves 1

4 ounces fresh fettuccine

1 ounce black truffle purée

$^1/_2$ ounce extra-virgin olive oil

$^1/_2$ ounce white truffle oil

$^1/_2$ ounce unsalted butter

Pinch of salt

1 ounce Reggiano Parmesan cheese, shaved

Pinch of parsley, minced

Drop fettuccine in a large pot of boiling salted water.

While pasta is cooking, mix all ingredients except parsley and cheese in a mixing bowl.

Drain pasta and toss with mixed ingredients.

Empty contents from mixing bowl, using a pasta fork to spin fettuccine, into the center of a large hot pasta bowl. Top pasta with shaved cheese and sprinkle minced parsley.

FOIE GRAS PIZZA

Serves 1

6 ounces pizza dough

1 ounce olive oil

2 ounces shredded mozzarella cheese

3 ounces Chianti onions

4 ounces fresh mozzarella cheese

1 Portobello mushroom cap, roasted

$^1/_2$ teaspoon fresh herbs

2 ounces foie gras, seared

$^1/_2$ ounce truffle oil

Roll out the pizza dough and spread olive oil to the edges. Place shredded mozzarella cheese on the bottom layer. Then place onions, followed by fresh mozzarella and thinly sliced Portobello mushroom. Sprinkle with mixed herbs and place into pizza oven.

Cook, turning frequently, until pizza is golden brown on all edges. Slice into four pieces. Slice seared foie gras on a bias into four pieces and place on each slice of pizza. Drizzle with truffle oil and place on a hot plate.

Lobster with Truffle Butter Sauce

Serves 4

4 1½-pound fresh lobsters
Truffle butter sauce (recipe follows)
20 asparagus spears, blanched
1 sprig Italian flat leaf parsley
Shaved Italian white truffles (optional)
1 ounce unsalted butter
Salt and pepper

In a large pot of heavily salted, boiling water, drop the live lobster in and cook for about 6 minutes (4 minutes per pound of lobster).

Pull lobster from water. Pull claws off and crack carefully, trying to keep them whole, and set aside. With a large knife, split lobster in half from head to tail.

Heat the asparagus spears in a sauté pan with butter, salt, and pepper to taste. Place the lobster on an entrée plate with the asparagus and claws. Drizzle with truffle butter sauce. Garnish with a sprig of Italian parsley. To truly make this a special dish, add fresh Italian white shaved truffles.

Truffle Butter Sauce

½ ounce, olive oil
4 shallots, minced
¼ cup rice vinegar
¼ cup heavy cream
2 cups unsalted butter at room temperature, cut into tablespoons
½ ounce white truffle oil
12 ounces black truffle slices packed in oil
Salt and pepper to taste

Place olive oil in a heavy-bottomed saucepot over medium-high heat Add minced shallots and sauté until translucent. Add rice vinegar and white wine and reduce until syrupy consistency. Add heavy cream and reduce until thick and syrupy.

Turn heat down to medium and begin to whisk in butter until fully incorporated. Finish sauce by adding truffle oil, sliced truffles, and salt and pepper.

Set the sauce aside until ready to use. Sauce must be kept in a warm place—not too hot or too cold or sauce will break.

Maison Dupuy

The Maison Dupuy, with its rich heritage and prime location, offers an authentic French Quarter experience that few other New Orleans hotels can equal. This hotel is nestled within the Vieux Carré, or "Old Square," the original seven square blocks along the Mississippi River established as the French Quarter in 1722. No new hotel rooms have been permitted in this exclusive region of New Orleans since 1972.

The Maison Dupuy has long stood as a prominent New Orleans landmark. It was built on the site of the nation's first cotton press, constructed by New Orleans' first elected mayor, John Pitot, in 1602. Eventually two brothers, Clarence and Milton Dupuy, purchased the site and transformed seven town homes into their magnificent family residence. The Maison Dupuy, or "House of Dupuy," soon became the most elegant home in the French Quarter. It maintains the largest and most beautiful courtyard in the Vieux Carré to this day.

The modern history of this French Quarter hotel continues to resonate with distinction. In 1997, the hotel declared the grand opening of Dominique's, the signature restaurant of nationally acclaimed restaurateur Dominique Macquet. It is also the former residence of Paul Prudhomme, who presided over the kitchen as its first chef 20 years ago.

Maison Dupuy

1001 Rue Toulousse

New Orleans, Louisiana 70130

(504) 586-8000

"One cannot think well, love well, sleep well, if one has not dined well."
Virginia Woolf

FIRE-ROASTED SHRIMP

WITH TOASTED PEANUT ORZO AND KAFFIR-LIME-GINGER FUMET WITH CRUNCHY VEGETABLES

Here is one of my all-time favorite dishes built around shrimp. It draws its heat from the Scotch bonnet pepper, an irregularly-shaped chile favored in the Caribbean that is closely related to the habanero. The dish's sweetness comes from its flirtation with Asian ingredients for the orzo. I particularly like what happens when you mix garam masala—the real Indian version of what we call curry powder—with the kaffir lime leaf and ginger broth.

Serves 4

Crunchy Vegetables

$1/2$ teaspoon salt

1 tablespoon freshly squeezed lime juice

1 teaspoon chile oil (recipe follows)

1 teaspoon sugar

2 cups julienned mixed vegetables, such as carrots, daikon, jicama, zucchini, squash

Salt and pepper

In a medium bowl, whisk together the salt, lime juice, chile oil, and sugar. Add the vegetables, and toss to coat. Season with pepper and additional salt to taste. (The vegetables will keep, covered, in the refrigerator for up to 1 hour. They are also delicious in a light salad.)

Chile Oil

1 bunch cilantro

1 large shallot

1 2-inch piece of fresh ginger, peeled

$1/2$ cup canola oil

$1/4$ cup sesame oil (not toasted)

3 seeded scotch bonnet peppers

Cut off the cilantro stems and set aside the leafy portion (to be used with Fire-Roasted Shrimp preparation). Put the stems in a small, non-reactive saucepan.

Trim and chop the shallot and set aside the chopped shallot. Add the trimmings to the cilantro stems.

Finely grate the ginger and place it in a square of cheesecloth. Twist to squeeze the ginger juice into another pan. Set aside the pan of juice. Add the pulp to the stems and trimmings.

Add the canola oil, sesame oil, and chiles to the pan of stems, trimmings, and pulp. Bring to a boil over medium heat.

Remove from the heat and let cool to room temperature. Strain through a fine sieve into a small container. Discard solids. Yields about ⅔ cup. (The oil will keep, covered, in the refrigerator for up to 2 weeks.)

Continued next page

Fire-Roasted Shrimp

1 pound shrimp (jumbo)

2 teaspoons chili oil

1 teaspoon sea salt

2 tablespoons coconut milk

1 tablespoon light soy sauce

2 tablespoons ginger juice (juicer-extracted)

1 teaspoon canola oil

1 small carrot, chopped

1 stalk celery, chopped

2 cups water

2 cloves garlic, chopped

2 Kaffir lime leaves, julienned

$\frac{1}{2}$ teaspoon garam masala or curry powder

$1\frac{1}{2}$ cups dry orzo pasta

$\frac{1}{2}$ cup crushed peanuts

$\frac{1}{4}$ cup peanut oil

Boil a large pot of salted water for cooking the orzo. Peel and de-vein the shrimp, leaving the tails intact. Reserve the shells and heads.

Chop enough of the reserved leafy portion of the cilantro to yield 6 tablespoons.

In a bowl, combine 2 tablespoons of the cilantro, the chile oil, and sea salt. Add the shrimp and toss to coat. Cover and set aside in the refrigerator.

Add the coconut milk and soy sauce to the ginger juice and set aside.

In a saucepan, heat the canola oil over medium heat. Add the carrots, celery,

and reserved chopped shallots. Cook about 3 minutes, until softened.

Add the water and bring to a boil. Add the reserved shrimp shells and heads, garlic, kaffir lime leaves, and garam masala. Decrease the heat to low and simmer uncovered for 20 minutes.

Transfer the shrimp-shell mixture to a blender or food processor and process until the shells are finely chopped. Strain and press through a fine sieve into a small saucepan. Retain the broth in the saucepan, discarding the solids.

Cook the orzo pasta in boiling water until al dente, 7–8 minutes. Drain.

Heat the peanut oil and sauté the crushed peanuts. Add to the orzo pasta. Mix in the ginger/coconut milk sauce and the chopped cilantro leaves from the chili oil.

Meanwhile, heat a large heavy skillet over high heat. Add the reserved marinated shrimp and sauté until they are opaque in the center, about 4 minutes.

To serve, reheat the coconut broth without boiling, if necessary, and add the remaining 3 tablespoons of cilantro. Mound orzo pasta in the center of each plate and pool shrimp broth around it. Arrange the shrimp over the broth. Garnish with crunchy vegetables.

Tujague's

Welcome to the second-oldest restaurant in New Orleans. Located in the heart of the French Quarter, facing the historic French Market, Tujague's has retained its reputation for providing an unforgettable dining experience in the original Creole tradition. In existence before "New Orleans" even bore its name, and having served as a Spanish armory, Tujague's restaurant has survived decades of war, depression, fire, and plague to bring its guests a tradition of culinary excellence that remains undiminished today.

Prosperity had never smiled more broadly on New Orleans than it did in the period when Tujague's first opened its doors. The city's growth during the 1850s was immense and, for European emigrants in search of success in the New World, opportunity was theirs for the taking.

Guillaume and Marie Abadie Tujague took advantage of this in 1852 when they married and set sail for America from Bordeaux, France. Guillaume Tujague became a butcher in the French Market for three years before they established Tujague's Restaurant in 1856. They began by serving breakfast and lunch to the dockworkers, market laborers, and seamen who crowded that part of the riverfront. The South was still recovering from the Civil War, but Tujague's never missed serving a meal.

The lunches were seven-course affairs, but the reputation of Tujague's from the beginning was built on two dishes: a piquant remoulade sauce flavoring spicy cold shrimp, and succulent chunks of beef brisket boiled with aromatic vegetables and served with a horseradish sauce. Horse and buggies still traveled on cobblestone streets outside of the restaurant, although an occasional automobile would be seen. Inside, a beer was only four cents.

Sometime before Guilliaume Tujague died in 1912, he sold the restaurant to Phlibert Guichet, who had come to work there from Guichetville, a community near Raceland in Lafourche Parish.

Tujague's closest competition always had been Begue's, a restaurant a few doors up Decatur at the corner of Madison. The proprietor-chef there was the legendary Elizabeth Kettenring Dutreuil Begue, a Bavarian emigrant who had been cooking for the French Market crowd since 1863.

Tujague's

823 Decatur Street

New Orleans, Louisiana 70130

(504) 525-8676

In 1906, Madame Begue died, and her restaurant was taken over by her daughter and son-in-law, the Anouilles.

One of the employees at Madame Begue's was Jean-Dominic Castet, who had come to New Orleans from France in 1905. Castet and Philibert Buichet decided to join forces, and in 1914 they bought Elizabeth Begue's restaurant from her now-widowed daughter and hung out a new sign reading "Tujague's." And Tujague's it's been ever since.

For older New Orleanians, the person most closely identified with Tujague's was the industrious Clemence Castet, Jean-Cominic's widow. Until her death in 1969, she ruled the dining room and the kitchen with an iron hand, often bringing food to the tables herself.

After Clemence Castet's death, the Guichet family retained ownership of Tujague's until 1982, when New Orleans businessman Steven Latter took it over. Latter has painstakingly researched the restaurant's history to restore it to its early state. In the dining room and the connecting saloon, which contains a bar brought from France in 1856, Latter has covered the walls with photos, clippings, and other memorabilia relating to the history of Tujague's.

Latter has resurrected many of the restaurant's culinary traditions as well.

Today, the customers are still served several traditional Tujague's specialties: shrimp remoulade, beef brisket with horseradish, "cap" bread (a Tujague's original), and dark coffee in shot glasses.

Tujague's long ago became a local institution, but New Orleans could never keep a good thing to herself. Inevitably, the pleasures of Tujague's were shared with visitors. Various presidents—Roosevelt, Truman, Eisenhower, and France's De Gaulle—have enjoyed Tujague's hospitality. The guest book also includes such notables as Cole Porter, O. Henry, Diane Sawyer, Don Johnson, Harrison Ford, Margot Kidder, Dan Akroyd, Ty Cobb, John D. Rockefeller, and other well-known personalities who appreciate fine food.

The restaurant's style is as refreshingly unpretentious as ever. It is unmistakably a New Orleans classic neighborhood restaurant. You'll think you've stepped back in time when you see the ancient mirror that graced a Paris bistro for ninety years before making the journey to New Orleans, or when you run your fingers across the famous cypress bar that survived prohibition. When you enter the restaurant and smell the aroma, you'll be enjoying the same sensations as did brunch guests of Madame Begue's "petite dejeuner" all those years ago—Tujague's serves up those same famous dishes today!

REMOULADE SAUCE

Yields 2 quarts

3 cups white onions, finely chopped

2 cups celery, finely chopped

1 cup green onion, finely chopped

1 cup fresh parsley, finely chopped

1 cup lettuce, finely chopped

16 ounces Creole mustard or brown mustard

1 1/2 pints olive oil

1/4 cup fresh lemon juice

Generous amount of paprika, for color

Salt and pepper to taste

Mix all chopped vegetables together. Add Creole mustard and mix well. Add paprika, olive oil, and salt and pepper to taste.

Note: Sauce can be made in advance and will keep for several days.

CRAB AND SPINACH BISQUE

Serves 10–12

4 10-ounce bags fresh spinach, finely chopped and set aside with its juice

2 cups butter

6 tablespoons flour

3/4 cup cream cheese

1 cup milk

2 pints whipping cream

1 pound crabmeat

1/2 24-ounce can chicken stock or 1 12-ounce can chicken bouillon

Melt butter in a large pot Add flour and stir until smooth, making sure there are no lumps. Add cream, crabmeat and chicken broth or bouillon. Add spinach and simmer.

Melt cream cheese on a slow fire until smooth. Add milk and stir. Add to soup and let cook for 5 minutes. Slowly add water until the bisque reaches desired consistency.

BOILED BEEF BRISKET

Serves 12–15

6–7 pounds choice brisket

2 onions, quartered

1 1/2 ribs of celery, quartered

1 head garlic, peeled

1 bay leaf

1 tablespoon salt

15 black peppercorns

2 green onions, quartered

1 carrot, quartered

1 bell pepper, quartered

Sauce

1 cup ketchup

1/2 cup horseradish

1/4 cup Creole mustard

Place the brisket in a large soup pot, cover with cold water, add all the ingredients and simmer for 3–4 hours until beef is tender.

Remove beef and slice.

For vegetable soup

Skim and strain the stock. Add 3 tablespoons tomato paste, 2 whole tomatoes sliced, and your favorite vegetables. Cook until tender and serve.

Note: We have found a little okra adds a distinctive taste to the soup. Cut and cook okra first in the oven or a saucepan to remove the slime before putting into the soup.

Any leftover stock can be frozen and stored for future soups and sauces.

The two most important steps to produce tender, juicy, tasty brisket are: 1) Buy a quality, well-trimmed brisket, never frozen; 2) Simmer the meat (not a hard boil).

Chateau Sonesta Hotel

Chateau Sonesta Hotel

800 Iberville Street

New Orleans, Louisiana 70112

(504) 565-4596

In the late 1830s and '40s, while searching to expand his booming business, Daniel Henry Holmes saw that there was a definite trend towards uptown New Orleans, the "new" section of the city. Not wanting to abandon the traditional commercial district in the "old" section of the city, he decided that his store needed a centralized location. Being a true innovator, Mr. Holmes selected a site in the primarily residential area of Canal Street for the simple reason that it was the widest thoroughfare in the city, perfectly situated between the "old" and the "new."

On October 15, 1849, Daniel Holmes opened one of the most important additions to Canal Street, the D.H. Holmes Department Store. In the beginning, the new store was operated by a staff of five employees. For the convenience of his customers the store stayed open at night until after the opera ended.

Holmes offered the finest lace goods, fans, ribbons, leather goods, jewelry, parasols, gloves, and a large fabric section, which he acquired on his buying trips to Europe. Here a lady could procure a complete summer, winter, bridal, mourning, or traveling outfit from Holmes' order and fitting department in a matter of days.

The D.H. Holmes Department Store operated for 140 years (from 1849 until 1989), became a local treasure, and gained a national reputation as one of the outstanding retail establishments in the United States. Upon the store's closing, the property was donated to the City of New Orleans. The city, in turn, created the Canal Street Development Corporation, a public benefit corporation formed to administer the project of rescuing the pre-Civil War structure.

The City of New Orleans, Historic Restoration Inc. (the developer), and Sonesta International Hotels Corporation united with a common mission in mind: to preserve and readapt the use of this historic building by turning it into a truly unique hotel. The 251-room luxury hotel opened in April 1995, a successful example of public/private partnership.

The transformation of the pre-Civil War landmark into a twentieth-century hotel included a complete interior renovation and exterior restoration to the building's

1913 facade. Many special reminders of the building's past have been incorporated into the hotel:

- Alabaster pillars from the original D.H. Holmes soda fountain adorn the bar in the Clock Bar.
- Marble accents in the floor of the lobby, as well as the iron (faux marble) columns in the lobby, were preserved from the original structure.
- The cypress exposed beams in the Atrium Courtyard date back to 1849 and were part of the original building.
- The famous clock, which was a favorite meeting place for generations of New Orleanians and had been missing since the store closed, was returned to the hotel in November of 1995 during a "D.H. Holmes Memorabilia Party" by two well-meaning "preservationists" who had disconnected the clock from its Canal Street perch for safekeeping. The clock presently hangs in its original location on Canal Street.
- Underneath the clock is the $23,000 bronze sculpture of Ignatius Reilly, funded jointly by the hotel and the Downtown Development District. The statue mimics the opening scene of the 1981 Pulitzer Prize-winning novel *A Confederacy of Dunces.* The comical character waits for his mother under the D.H. Holmes clock, clutching a Werlein's shopping bag and dressed in a hunting cap, flannel shirt, baggy pants, and scarf.

STRAWBERRY BALSAMICO SWIRLED CHEESECAKE

Yields 1 cheesecake

Cheesecake

5 cups cream cheese at room temperature

1 $^3/_4$ cups granulated sugar

3 tablespoons all-purpose flour

Zest of 1 lemon

Zest of 1 orange

$^1/_4$ teaspoon vanilla extract

5 eggs

2 additional egg yolks

$^1/_4$ cup whipping cream

9-inch springform pan, greased generously with
   butter and patted with graham cracker crumbs

Strawberry Balsamico Jam

4 $^1/_2$ cups fresh strawberries

1 bottle (16 $^3/_4$ ounces) balsamic vinegar

$^1/_2$ cup granulated sugar

$^1/_4$ cup port wine

Heat oven to 500 degrees.

Prepare springform pan.

With an electric beater, mix the cream cheese, sugar, flour, orange and lemon zests, and vanilla until smooth. Add the eggs and the 2 additional egg yolks, beating in one at a time, and then add cream.

Strawberry Balsamico Jam

Place cleaned and de-stemmed strawberries into a saucepan with sugar, balsamic vinegar, and port. Cook over low to medium heat for about 20–30 minutes. Pour mixture into a blender and purée. Let cool. Set aside in a bowl for serving with cheesecake.

Pour the cream cheese mixture into prepared springform pan and spoon strawberry jam mixture over the top and into the cheesecake. Swirl it around with a toothpick, skewer, knife, etc. Bake for 10 minutes or until top of cake turns golden brown.

Reduce oven temperature to 200–225 degrees and bake for one hour longer.

Remove cake from oven and cool on a rack until it reaches room temperature. Then release the sides of the pan. Do not remove the bottom of the pan. Place cake on a platter. Ladle jam over cheesecake or each serving. Enjoy!

Barbecued Shrimp
with Mirliton Slaw

Serves 2

Slaw

2 mirliton (chayote squash)

2 tablespoons mayonnaise

2 tablespoons buttermilk

1 tablespoon sour cream

1 tablespoon yellow onion, finely diced

1–2 teaspoons fresh tarragon, diced

Peel the mirliton with a paring knife, cut in half, and remove pit. Use a mandolin or shredder to cut the mirliton into small juliennes.

Mix the remaining ingredients to create a sauce.

In a bowl, toss the mirliton with enough of the sauce to lightly coat it (the sauce will pull moisture from the mirliton, leaving it thin and runny, so do not add too much). Set in refrigerator until ready to plate up.

Shrimp

6 large shrimp (peeled and de-veined with tail fin on)

1 teaspoon shallots, chopped

1 teaspoon garlic, minced

$^1/_2$ teaspoon fresh thyme leaves

$^1/_2$ teaspoon fresh oregano, chopped

$^1/_2$ teaspoon fresh rosemary, chopped

Salt and fresh cracked black pepper

2 ounces dry white wine

2 tablespoons Worcestershire sauce

Dash hot sauce

6 tablespoons whole butter (cut into pieces)

Place a sauté pan on high heat and allow to heat thoroughly. Drop about 1 ounce of the butter pieces into pan until it just starts to brown. Sauté the shallot and garlic and flip in pan for 4–5 seconds. Add the shrimp to the pan and sprinkle with the fresh herbs and salt and pepper. Toss shrimp in the pan to get a little color on them. Add in the white wine, Worcestershire and hot sauce then let reduce to about half. Swirl in the whole butter, and test the shrimp for doneness.

To serve, divide the slaw on the center of two plates (squeeze lightly to relieve excess moisture). Arrange three shrimp radially symmetrically around the slaw on each plate. Spoon a little of the butter sauce over and around the shrimp. (For more visual effect, lightly drizzle drops of the slaw sauce over the butter sauce). Garnish with chives and serve with sliced baguette.

This is ideally done as an appetizer, although it can be extended into a light entrée. Remember to use gloves when preparing raw mirliton or you will get a scaly covering on your hands that may last for two to three days—not very romantic. The shrimp is barbecued New Orleans-style in a pan with a Worcestershire- and rosemary-flavored sauce instead of being grilled.

Bourbon House

Bourbon House

144 Bourbon

New Orleans, Louisiana 70130

(504) 522-0111

www.bourbonhouse.com

Dickie Brennan grew up in the kitchen at Commander's Palace, which was run by his father, Dick, and his Aunt Ella. So that his parent's generation could begin to retire from the business, Dickie was afforded the opportunity to purchase the Palace Café in 1994, a restaurant that Dickie and his cousins opened in the French Quarter in 1991. A few years later, Dickie opened his now nationally ranked Dickie Brennan's Steakhouse in 1998. In 2002, he opened Bourbon House.

Built over the site of a former Woolworth's store, Bourbon House's handcrafted wrought iron, traditional bentwood chairs, long-leaf pine floors, and custom millwork are all indicative of New Orleans' European heritage. "The look and feel of this restaurant have evolved from my love of French brasseries. I always wanted to open a restaurant that captured this same feeling, but to imprint it with the personality of New Orleans. It had to be authentic. With Bourbon House, we've realized this dream," Dickie Brennan said.

The casual elegance carries over from the restaurant's main dining room, which seats 230 people, to the oyster bar and mezzanine-level private dining rooms. Chicago-based award-winning restaurant designer/architect Mark Knauer (who also designed Palace Café and Dickie Brennan's Steakhouse) worked closely with New Orleans-based Williams & Associates in the restaurant's design. Leslie Brennan, Dickie Brennan's wife, guided the interior design of Bourbon House.

Bourbon House utilizes classic cooking techniques with Gulf fish entrées ranging from Redfish on the Half Shell (grilled skin-on) to Baked Fish Greig (with jumbo lump crabmeat and Creole meunière) to the pan-sautéed Gulf Fish Iberville (with a sauté of Gulf shrimp, oysters, fresh artichokes, and mushrooms) and crispy, fried Des Allemandes catfish. With Shrimp Chippewa, a nearly forgotten New Orleans classic returns.

Bourbon House boasts an impressive collection of small batch and single barrel bourbons and a signature Frozen Bourbon Milk Punch. Bourbon House is owned and operated by Dickie Brennan, Lauren Brennan Brower and Steve Pettus, who also own and operate the Palace Café and Dickie Brennan's Steakhouse.

According to *The New York Times*, "if you're up for a more casual experience, belly up to the oyster bar at the Bourbon House and slurp down a dozen fresh-shucked beauties washed down with a fizzy local beer or the house specialty cocktail, a frozen bourbon milk punch topped with a sprinkle of nutmeg. Located mere feet away from Bourbon Street's high-octane chaos, the room's huge windows make this raw bar one of the best people-watching perches in the city."

CRAWFISH RAVIGOTE

Serves 8

¹/₂ cup mayonnaise

¹/₄ cup Creole mustard

¹/₂ tablespoon capers, chopped

³/₄ teaspoon prepared horseradish

1 hard-boiled egg, chopped

2 green onions (green parts only), thinly sliced

1 pound cooked crawfish

¹/₄ cup olive oil

2 tablespoons cane vinegar

1 head green leaf lettuce, sliced into very thin ribbons

1 carrot, julienned

¹/₄ small head purple cabbage, thinly sliced

Salt and fresh ground pepper to taste

Fold together the mayonnaise, Creole mustard, capers, horseradish and half of both the chopped egg and green onion in a non-reactive bowl. Adjust seasoning with salt and fresh ground pepper to taste.

Season crawfish tails with salt and fresh ground pepper. Gently fold in the ravigote dressing.

Blend together the oil and vinegar and season to taste with salt and fresh ground pepper. Toss the lettuce, carrots, and cabbage with the vinaigrette.

To serve, divide the salad onto chilled serving plates. Top each with about 4 ounces of the crawfish ravigote. Garnish with the remaining chopped egg and thinly sliced green onions.

DEVILED STUFFED CRAB

Served on local squash and Amite tomato ratatouille and drizzled with Creole meunière (recipes follow.)

Serves 4–6

1 cup unsalted butter
1 teaspoon garlic, minced
2 stalks celery, chopped
1/4 cup bell pepper, chopped
1/4 cup yellow onion, chopped
1 teaspoon dried thyme
1 pound blue crab claw meat
1/4 bunch green onion, chopped
2 tablespoons Romano cheese
1/2 cup fresh French breadcrumbs
1 tablespoon Creole Seasoning
Chopped parsley and lemon slices for garnish
Cleaned crab shells

Melt the butter in a medium sauté pan. Add garlic, celery, bell pepper, onion, and thyme, and sauté until tender. Fold in the crabmeat and green onion. Cook for five more minutes.

Combine the Romano cheese, breadcrumbs, and Creole seasoning.

Spoon the crabmeat stuffing into clean crab shells and sprinkle with the breadcrumb topping. Bake at 350 degrees for 10 minutes, or until golden brown.

Ratatouille

1 squash
1 zucchini
1 red onion
1 eggplant (small)
3 tomatoes
1 cup vegetable juice
1 cup fresh tender herbs (e.g., parsley, basil, sage)
Kosher salt and cracked black pepper to taste

Cut the vegetables into uniform shapes (e.g., batonnet or cubes). Sauté just until tender, then stir in the vegetable juice and fresh herbs. Season to taste.

Meunière Sauce

1 lemon, peeled and quartered
1/2 cup Worcestershire Sauce
1/2 cup hot pepper sauce
1/4 cup heavy whipping cream
2 cups butter, cold, cut into small cubes
Kosher salt and white pepper to taste

Combine the lemon, Worcestershire sauce and hot sauce in a heavy saucepot. Reduce over medium heat, stirring constantly with a wire whisk until mixture becomes thick and syrupy. Whisk in the heavy whipping cream.

Reduce heat to low and slowly blend in the butter one cube at a time, adding additional butter only after previously added butter has been completely incorporated into the sauce.

Remove from heat and continue to stir. Season with salt and pepper to taste. Strain through a fine strainer and keep warm.

"*The discovery of a new dish does more for the happiness of mankind than the discovery of a new star.*"
Anthelme Brillat-Savarin

The Court of Two Sisters

The Court of Two Sisters

613 Royal Street

New Orleans, Louisiana 70130

(504) 522-7261

www.courtoftwosisters.com

It was two Creole sisters and the notions shop they owned on this site that gave The Court of Two Sisters its name. However, 613 Rue Royale has long played a significant role in the history of the French Quarter and old New Orleans.

Originally known as "Governor's Row," the 600 block of Rue Royale was home to five governors, two state Supreme Court Justices, a future Justice of the U.S. Supreme Court, and a future President of the United States. It is not surprising, then, that the original resident of 613 Rue Royale was Sieur Etienne de Perier, royal governor of colonial Louisiana between 1726 and 1733. It has also been rumored that the outrageous Marquis de Vaudreuil, the colonial royal governor who transformed New Orleans from a marshland village into a "petit Paris," was once a resident of 613 Rue Royale.

The two sisters, Emma and Bertha Camors, born 1858 and 1860 respectively, belonged to a proud and aristocratic Creole family. Their "rabais," or notions, outfitted many of the city's finest women with formal gowns, lace, and perfumes imported from Paris.

Marriage, reversals of fortune, widowhood—nothing could separate the sisters. Indeed, as the *Picayune* was to report, the sisters died within two months of each other in the winter of 1944. United in death as in life, the sisters lie side by side at St. Louis Cemetery #3.

In an interesting twist of fate, ownership has passed to two brothers. Joseph Fein, III explains, "Someone asks me about the two sisters every day. They are surprised to hear that my brother and I are not related to the two sisters, yet we own and run The Court of Two Sisters. I explain that after the two sisters died, ownership changed hands many times until it reached our father, Joe Fein, Jr., who guided what had become a restaurant onto its current path—a path my brother, Jerry, and I work hard to maintain with the highest quality food and service. We will continue what the two sisters and our father did best: entertain[ing] visitors in the largest courtyard in the French Quarter with a memorable dining experience."

Brother Jerome Fein says, "New Orleans is a destination for food, history, and music. The Court of Two Sisters offers an authentic blend of all. Guests from all over compliment us on the quality of all our food—from the hot and cold buffets to our gourmet Creole dinners. Our picturesque old-world courtyard with original gas lights and flowing fountains and our three different[ly-]styled dining rooms add to the unique history of our French Quarter building.

"We are proud to be the only historic restaurant in New Orleans to offer a strolling trio playing real New Orleans jazz seven days a week during our world-famous Daily Jazz Brunch.

"My brother and I are committed to maintaining the reputation of The Court of Two Sisters as one of New Orleans' premier restaurants."

SHRIMP TOULOUSE

Serves 6

2 pounds 36–40 count shrimp,
   peeled and de-veined
1 pound butter, softened
1 1/2 cup mushrooms, sliced
1/2 cup green bell pepper, small diced
1/2 cup red bell pepper, small diced
1/2 cup green onions, sliced
2 teaspoons Toulouse seasoning
   (Creole seasoning)
3/4 cup white wine

Heat 2 ounces of butter in a large sauté pan. Add mushrooms, green, and red bell peppers and sauté until clear. Add green onions, shrimp, and Toulouse seasoning and sauté until shrimp start to turn pink. Add white wine and reduce liquid by half.

When liquid is reduced, swirl butter, about 3 ounces at a time, over low heat. When all butter is incorporated, remove from heat and serve over white rice.

"All happiness depends on a leisurely breakfast."
John Gunther

CHOCOLATE ESPRESSO TORTE
WITH WHITE CHOCOLATE GANACHE AND RASPBERRY COULIS

Torte

2 cups lightly salted butter, softened

12 ounces semi-sweet chocolate

4 ounces unsweetened chocolate

7 ounces sugar

2 ounces espresso coffee grinds

2 ounces water

2 ounces Grand Marnier

12 each eggs

Put butter, chocolates, sugar, coffee, and water in top of double boiler on medium heat. Heat and stir until chocolate and butter are melted. Let cool.

Put eggs into a bowl and beat slightly. Add chocolate mixture and Grand Marnier. Pour into buttered cake pan and bake in water bath at 350 degrees for 1 hour.

Remove from oven and refrigerate at least 2 hours to cool. Invert pan to remove.

White Chocolate Ganache

1 pound white chocolate, chopped

1 cup cream

2 ounces lightly salted butter

Heat in double boiler until melted and keep warm.

Raspberry Coulis

2 pints fresh raspberries, rinsed

$\frac{1}{2}$ cup sugar

1 ounce water

Heat until sugar is dissolved. Remove from heat and purée, strain and chill.

Slice torte into 12 portions. Put 2 ounces white chocolate ganache onto serving plate. Put torte in center and drizzle with raspberry coulis.

Mr. B's Bistro

Mr. B's Bistro
201 Royal Street
New Orleans, Louisiana 70130
(504) 523-2078
www.mrbsbistro.com

Nestled in the heart of the French Quarter, Mr. B's Bistro is located at the intersection of Royal Street and Iberville, one of New Orleans' most celebrated food corners. Since the 1860s, this corner has been a New Orleans landmark. In 1868, this once-quiet corner was transformed into Solari's Market. New Orleanians came from all over town to visit this soda fountain and lunch counter which also specialized in merchandise not found anywhere else, such as out-of-season fruits and vegetables, rare liquors, exquisite candy, and imported cookies. Solari's closed its doors for the final time in 1965, but fourteen years later, in 1979, John, Ella, Dick, Dottie, and Adelaide Brennan resurrected this celebrated food corner into Mr. B's and beckoned the culinary world inside.

Since 1979, Mr. B's has been an integral part of the ongoing process of redefining New Orleans cooking. Louisiana Cuisine is a melting pot of diverse cultures, including French, Spanish, Italian, African, American Indian,

> *"Wine brings to light the hidden secrets of the soul."*
> Horace

and Caribbean. New Orleans' location and growth as a port city has allowed these various cultures to blend together harmoniously, utilizing the foods of South Louisiana, to create a style of cooking referred to as "Creole Cuisine." Mr. B's has attempted to revive the distinct qualities of Louisiana's varied cultural influences, adapting and incorporating local and regional ingredients into innovative culinary creations. Quality and farm freshness predominate; homemade sausages, cured and smoked meats, pickles, and chutneys are evidence of the restaurant's dedication to distinction.

Mr. B's is proud to offer regional Creole cuisine strong in its flavorful ties both to New Orleans and to South Louisiana. It embraces the challenge for simple and honest food in a "bistro" style. For an all-occasion business lunch, a festive jazz brunch or dinner accompanied by live piano music, Mr. B's strives to deliver a great dining experience to its guests.

JUMBO LUMP CRABCAKES

There are crabcakes, and then there are Mr. B's crabcakes. Ours are so good because they're primarily crabmeat, with a just enough breadcrumbs and mayonnaise to hold the mixture together. We serve them all day long—they're brunch under poached eggs with hollandaise, they're lunch with a salad, and they make a great starter for dinner. We recommend using Japanese breadcrumbs called panko here for their incredible lightness. You can find them in specialty food markets and Asian markets. Fine dried breadcrumbs can be used in their place, but the cakes won't be as light.

Yields 8 cakes

1 pound jumbo lump crabmeat, picked over
$\frac{1}{2}$ medium red bell pepper, finely diced
$\frac{1}{2}$ medium green bell pepper, finely diced
$\frac{1}{3}$ cup mayonnaise
$\frac{1}{4}$ cup Panko breadcrumbs
3 scallions, thinly sliced
Juice of $\frac{1}{4}$ lemon
$\frac{1}{4}$ teaspoon Crystal hot sauce
$\frac{1}{4}$ teaspoon Creole seasoning
$\frac{1}{2}$ cup all-purpose flour
$\frac{1}{2}$ teaspoon salt
$\frac{1}{4}$ teaspoon freshly ground black pepper
2 tablespoons unsalted butter
Ravigote sauce as accompaniment

In a large bowl, combine crabmeat, bell peppers, mayonnaise, breadcrumbs, scallions, lemon juice, hot sauce, and Creole seasoning, being careful not to break up crabmeat lumps. Using a round cookie cutter (2½ inches by 1 inch), fill cutter with mixture and form into cakes. Place on a baking sheet. Chill cakes, uncovered, for 1 hour to help set.

Combine flour, salt, and pepper on a plate and lightly dust cakes in flour. In a large skillet, melt 1 tablespoon butter. Add half of cakes and cook over moderate heat until golden brown, about 1½ minutes on each side. Cook the remaining cakes in the same manner. Serve cakes with ravigote sauce (recipe follows).

Ravigote Sauce
Yields 1 $\frac{1}{2}$ cups

2 $\frac{1}{2}$ teaspoons fresh lemon juice
$\frac{1}{2}$ teaspoon dry mustard
1 $\frac{1}{4}$ cups mayonnaise
$\frac{1}{2}$ red bell pepper, finely diced
$\frac{1}{2}$ large Anaheim chile pepper or green bell pepper, finely diced
1 hard-boiled egg, diced
1 tablespoon flat leaf parsley, finely chopped
2 $\frac{3}{4}$ teaspoons prepared horseradish
1 $\frac{1}{4}$ teaspoon Dijon mustard
$\frac{3}{4}$ teaspoon dried tarragon
$\frac{3}{4}$ teaspoon hot sauce
Kosher salt and white pepper to taste

In a medium bowl, whisk together lemon juice and dry mustard. Whisk in mayonnaise, bell pepper, chile, egg, parsley, horseradish, mustard, tarragon, hot sauce, salt, and pepper.

Note: This sauce is New Orleans through and through. It can be served with all sorts of seafood: boiled shrimp and crab, crawfish, fried oysters, and crabcakes.

CREOLE BREAD PUDDING
WITH IRISH WHISKEY SAUCE

Serves 12

Bread pudding

¾ pound light, airy French bread, cut into
   1½-inch-thick slices

1 cup dark raisins

2 dozen large eggs

1½ quarts heavy cream

2½ cups sugar

1 tablespoon plus 1 teaspoon cinnamon

1 teaspoon ground nutmeg

¼ cup (½ stick) unsalted butter, chopped

Arrange half of the bread in a 13-inch by 9-inch baking pan and sprinkle with raisins. Arrange the remaining half of bread over top.

In a large bowl, whisk together eggs, cream, 2 cups sugar, 1 tablespoon cinnamon, and nutmeg until smooth. Pour half of custard over bread and gently press down bread. Let sit until bread soaks up custard, about 15 minutes (depending on bread). Pour remaining half of custard over bread and gently press down bread.

In a small bowl, combine remaining ½ cup sugar and teaspoon cinnamon and sprinkle over bread. Dot bread with butter and bake 1½–2 hours, or until custard is just set in the center.

Whiskey sauce

1 cup heavy cream

1 cup whole milk

½ cup sugar

7 large egg yolks

¼ cup Irish whiskey

Preheat an oven to 250 degrees.

In a medium saucepan, bring cream and milk to a boil.

In a medium bowl, whisk together sugar and yolks until combined well and gradually whisk in hot milk mixture.

Transfer mixture to a double boiler and cook over just simmering water, stirring gently but constantly with a rubber spatula or wooden spoon until thick, about 12 minutes. Pour sauce through a fine sieve and stir in whiskey. Serve sauce warm or cold.

If chilling sauce, let sauce become completely cold before covering, as condensation will cause it to thin. The sauce can be covered and chilled for up to 3 days. Makes 2¾ cups sauce.

Serve pudding warm, drizzled with whiskey sauce. Makes one 13- by 9-inch baking pan.

Forever thrifty in the kitchen, New Orleans cooks would never dream of wasting good, but stale French bread. Over the years, bread pudding has become our city's favorite dessert.

New Orleans bread is light and airy with a very tender crust that softens in this bread pudding. We could recommend other breads, but the bread pudding won't be like the one we serve at Mr. B's. Different breads absorb custard differently—your final result could be more custard-y or drier.

Arnaud's

In 1918, a colorful French wine salesman named Arnaud Cazenave opened the grand restaurant that bears his name. Count Arnaud (as he came to be called, without any bona fide claim to the title) practiced a brilliant new approach to the serving of food and drink.

Arnaud believed, quite simply, that the pursuit of the pleasures of the table is as worthy as anything else one does in life. For him, a meal that was only a meal was a shamefully wasted opportunity for enhancing one's life. This concept played very well to celebration-minded New Orleans. The following commentary is the Count's "Philosophy of Dining":

"Americans are prone to forget, in the ultra-rapidity and super-activity of modern life, trying to crowd eighty seconds of toil into a minute's time, that eating should be a pleasure, not a task to get over with in a hurry. A dinner chosen according to one's needs, tastes, and moods, well prepared and well served, is a joy to all senses and an impelling incentive to sound sleep, good health, and long life. Therefore, at least once a day, preferably in the quiet cool of the evening, one should throw all care to the winds, relax completely, and dine leisurely and well."

Just before Count Arnaud died, he let it be known that his successor was not to be his sheltered wife, Lady Irma, but his anything-but-sheltered daughter, Germaine. She was lusty, dramatic, loud, and headstrong. Her taste and capacity for alcohol, celebration, and men were extreme.

Germaine had a way of attracting attention, and she adored the spotlight. She defined the restaurant business as theatre. "It's a play in two acts," she said, "lunch and dinner." She took to the mock-royal rituals of Mardi Gras like a fish to water. She ruled over 22 Carnival balls, an over-achievement unlikely to be equaled. She instituted a parade of her own on Easter Sunday to show off her latest hats, with her friends following in horse-drawn buggies. That pageant continued after Germaine's death and persists to this day.

Arnaud's was the undisputed leading restaurant of New Orleans in the '30s and '40s. Arnaud's was where one went for any occasion that demanded

Arnaud's

813 Rue Bienville

New Orleans, Louisiana 70112

(866) 230-8895

94

celebration. The Count channeled much of its fortune into buying one adjoining property after another until Arnaud's 13 buildings (some of which had previously housed reputed opium dens and houses of prostitution) covered most of the block.

Stories emanated on a nightly basis about what went on at Arnaud's as its patrons pursued their sensual pleasures. Many tales from the early days concern Arnaud's various circumventions of Prohibition. Arnaud believed that wine and spirits are natural companions of good food and good living. The fact that they were illegal seemed but a detail.

Nevertheless, the law finally caught up with the Count. He was imprisoned and the restaurant padlocked for a time. Ultimately, he won the jury over, just in time for the end of Prohibition.

Germaine maintained in her mind the image of Arnaud's as one of the great restaurants of the world. Only the threat of impending financial ruin forced her hand. She agreed to lease the property and name of Arnaud's Restaurant to Archie Casbarian. On February 28, 1979, the renovated dining room reopened and a long renaissance of Arnaud's began. The man in charge, Archie Casbarian, was known for great restaurants.

Arnaud's needed all the creativity and managerial wherewithal that Casbarian

could bring to it. The place was a wreck. But Casbarian was committed to the idea that the new Arnaud's should look like Arnaud's, not like a new restaurant. The original chandeliers, iron columns, and cypress paneling were kept.

The wall of pebbled-glass windows was replaced by beautiful beveled glass, but the spirit was the same. During the renovation, a small section of the original tin ceiling was found and replicated to cover the entire main dining room. Silver, glassware, and china patterns remained the same as those originally chosen by the Count back in 1918. Most importantly, the original Italian tiles that covered the floors were left intact.

Arnaud's old customers are largely to thank for the faithfulness of the restoration. When the Richelieu Bar was rebuilt, it was authentic right down to the inconspicuous private street entrance. But some of the old-timers noticed something was missing: the "stoopie bench," previously used by over-indulging customers for a little lie-down before they returned to the outside world. The stoopie bench was quickly retrieved and restored.

Casbarian insists that, while new dishes are essential to the restaurant's growth, they must fit in with the Creole cuisine for which Arnaud's is celebrated.

Arnaud's Crème Brûlée

Serves 6

6 egg yolks
⅓ cup white sugar
2 ½ cups heavy cream
1 tablespoon vanilla extract
3 tablespoons dark brown sugar

Preheat the oven to 250 degrees.

In a medium bowl with mixer set at medium speed, beat the egg yolks and white sugar. Set aside.

In a saucepan over medium heat, bring the cream to a boil. Remove from heat immediately and add to the egg-sugar mixture, continuing to beat. Add the vanilla and continue to beat until the mixture is completely cool.

Pour the cooled mixture into 6 4-ounce custard cups. Line the sides of a 3-inch-high baking pan with parchment paper, then place the cups in the pan. Add water until it reaches halfway up the sides of the cups (The paper stabilizes the water and prevents the cups from shaking).

Bake for 50 minutes. Remove the cups from the pan, allow to cool to room temperature, then refrigerate until chilled.

Sprinkle ½ tablespoon dark brown sugar over the top of each cup. Place the cups on a sheet pan and set under the broiler until the sugar melts, darkens and forms a crust. This is the brûlée process. Refrigerate until ready to serve.

ROAST DUCK
WITH BALSAMIC VINEGAR GLAZE

Serves 4

1 cup balsamic vinegar

2 tablespoons honey

⅓ cup dried currants

1 teaspoon cayenne pepper

4 whole duck breasts, 6–8 ounces each

Salt and freshly ground pepper to taste

3 tablespoons pine nuts, toasted on stove top
   or in 350-degree oven for 4 minutes

Combine the vinegar, honey, currants, and cayenne in a small pot. Bring to a boil, lower heat to a simmer and reduce by half to form a thick syrupy glaze. Remove from heat and set aside.

With the point of a knife, score the skin side of the duck breasts in a crosshatch pattern, taking care not to pierce the flesh. Season with salt and pepper.

Heat a sauté pan over medium heat for 2 minutes before adding the breasts, skin-side down. Cook for approximately 6–8 minutes to render the fat. Carefully remove the excess fat from the sauté pan, then turn the breasts over and sauté the flesh side 3–4 minutes, until medium rare. Remove from the pan and slice lengthwise or crosswise.

Reheat the glaze. Arrange several slices of breast on each serving plate and drizzle with glaze, then sprinkle with toasted pine nuts.

G.W. Fins

G.W. Fins

808 Bienville

New Orleans, Louisiana 70112

(504) 581-FINS

www.gwfins.com

G.W. Fins is housed in a building constructed in the 1920s to serve as a loading area for the D.H. Holmes Department Store. The store was so large that when it closed in 1989, the property was ultimately converted into the Chateau Sonesta Hotel (see separate story), the Red Fish Grill and Zydecos. Holmes and its rival, Maison Blanche, were the Macy's and Gimbel's of New Orleans until they closed. The Ritz Carlton is now located in the Maison Blanche building.

The G.W. Fins building eventually transitioned into a department store itself, selling discount merchandise. Later, it would house a restaurant and ice cream shops. Folks from the suburbs would take cable cars downtown just to enjoy the food.

Located in the heart of the historic French Quarter, G.W. Fins ensures the highest-quality seafood by flying in products from around the globe and featuring only the best from local waters. G.W. Fins prints its menu daily in order to fulfill its ongoing commitment to freshness, variety, and customer satisfaction.

Locally owned and operated by Gary Wollerman and his partner, Executive Chef Tenney Flynn (who was named *New Orleans* magazine's "2004 Chef of the Year"), G.W. Fins' menu features popular dishes such as lobster dumplings, wood-grilled sea scallops with a wild mushroom risotto, cashew peppercorn swordfish, and individually prepared apple pie with a cheddar cheese straw crust and fresh vanilla bean ice cream.

Open for dinner seven nights a week, G.W. Fins tops *Southern Living's* list as one of "Our Ten Favorite Romantic Restaurants," with an ambience that is sophisticated yet comfortable. From romantic meals for two to corporate business dinners for ten, the service at G.W. Fins is regarded as some of the best in New Orleans. Private dining is also available. Reservations are recommended.

Experience the cuisine that earned G.W. Fins *Esquire* magazine's esteemed "Top 20 Best New Restaurants in America" award and a "4 bean" rating in the *New Orleans Times-Picayune*.

G.W. Fins is located two blocks into the French Quarter from Canal Street, nestled between Bourbon and Dauphine Streets.

MASHED SWEET POTATOES
WITH BANANAS AND VANILLA

3 pounds sweet potatoes, peeled and cut
   2-inch cubes

3 ripe bananas, peeled and sliced

1 cup heavy cream

1 small vanilla bean, split and scraped

$^1/_4$ cup honey

$^1/_2$ cup light brown sugar

3 tablespoons freshly squeezed orange juice

3 teaspoons salt

1 tablespoon Maker's Mark Bourbon

1 tablespoon soft butter

2 quarts water

Bring water and 2 teaspoons salt to a boil. Add the potatoes and cook until tender (about 15–20 minutes).

While potatoes are cooking, combine the cream, honey, brown sugar, split vanilla bean, bananas, and orange juice in a separate pot. Bring to a boil and cook on high for 5 minutes. Scrape vanilla bean and either purée the mixture with a mixing wand or mash well with a potato masher.

When the potatoes are tender, drain well and add to the cream mixture. Cook on medium heat for 4–5 minutes and mash gently with a spoon leaving some chunks of potato. The mixture will thicken slightly as the potatoes absorb the cream. Stir in the bourbon and the soft butter.

WHOLE ROASTED B-LINE SNAPPER
WITH MIDORI MANGO SLAW AND CARMELIZED BANANA

Mango Slaw

2 ripe mangos

$\frac{1}{2}$ of a ripe cantaloupe

$\frac{1}{2}$ of a ripe honeydew melon

1 tablespoon chopped mint

2 tablespoon chopped cilantro

2 tablespoons honey

$\frac{1}{2}$ cup seasoned rice vinegar

$\frac{1}{4}$ teaspoon Thai chili paste

2 ounces Midori melon liqueur

Cut the mango and melons in a long thin julienne.

Mix together remaining ingredients and stir until the honey is dissolved. Toss in the fruit and refrigerate for 15 minutes.

Snapper

1 $\frac{1}{2}$–2 pound whole snapper

Kosher salt

Freshly ground black pepper

2 tablespoons shallots, diced

1 tablespoon garlic, diced

2 tablespoons fine herbs, chopped (70% parsley, 20% chervil, 10% chives)

1 medium banana

4 tablespoons raw sugar

1 banana (or ginger) leaf

Scale and lightly score a 1½–2 pound whole snapper with a very sharp knife or a single-edged razor blade. Season liberally inside and out with salt, freshly ground black pepper, diced shallots, diced garlic, and chopped fine herbs.

Place the fish standing up in an oiled pie tin so that the tail and head are curving towards each other. Place in a 400-degree oven for about 15 minutes. To check for doneness, insert a pairing knife along the back bone and place it on your wrist. If it's hot, the fish are done.

Cut a banana in half and split it to make four pieces. Place in an oiled pie tin and cook at 400 degrees for 5 minutes.

Remove banana from oven and sprinkle a tablespoon of raw sugar on each piece. Caramelize under the broiler or with a torch.

Line a large plate with a banana or ginger leaf and place the cooked fish carefully on it. Garnish with the bananas and slaw.

"*The noblest of all dogs is the hot dog;
it feeds the hand that bites it.*"

Laurence J. Peter

Hotel Monteleone

Antonio Monteleone was an industrious nobleman operating a successful shoe factory in Sicily when the call of adventure motivated him to pack the tools of his trade and head for America, "the land of opportunity." Antonio arrived in New Orleans circa 1880 and opened a cobbler shop on Royal Street, the busy thoroughfare of commerce and banking in America's most European city. At the time, Royal Street was the grand street of the "Vieux Carré," as the French Colonials sometimes called the new town.

In 1886, Mr. Monteleone bought a 64-room hotel on the corner of Royal and Iberville streets in New Orleans' world-famous French Quarter. The setting was ripe for Antonio to spread his entrepreneurial wings when the nearby Commercial Hotel became available for purchase. That was only the beginning of an amazing historical landmark that is one of the last great family-owned and operated hotels in the city. Since 1886, four generations of Monteleones have dedicated themselves to maintaining their hotel, a sparkling jewel in the heart of the French Quarter.

There have been five major additions to the Hotel Monteleone. The first was in 1903 when 30 rooms were added. 300 more rooms were added in 1908, during a time of financial panic in the United States. The name of the hotel was also changed at this time, from the Commercial Hotel to Hotel Monteleone. In 1913, Antonio Monteleone passed away and was succeeded by his son Frank, who added 200 more rooms in 1928, a year before another horrible crash in the U.S. economy. The Hotel Monteleone was one of America's few family-owned hotels to weather the depression. It remained unchanged until 1954, when a fourth addition required the razing of the original building. The foundation was laid for a completely new building that would include guest facilities, ballrooms, dining rooms, and cocktail lounges. In 1964, under the direction of Bill Monteleone, who took over after his father passed in 1958, more floors, guestrooms, and a Sky Terrace with swimming pools and cocktail lounges were added.

Hotel Monteleone

214 Royal Street

New Orleans, Louisiana 70130

(504) 523-3341

www.hotelmonteleone.com

The Carousel Bar is the only revolving bar in New Orleans. It overlooks famous Royal Street through large fan windows and has long been a favorite of locals and tourists alike.

Several icons of the literary world have been great fans of the hotel. The famous novelist and playwright Truman Capote was fond of telling interviewers that he was born at the Hotel Monteleone. Actually, his mother stayed at the hotel leading up to his birth and the hotel staff transported her to Touro Infirmary, where the birth actually took place.

Ernest Hemingway covered the Spanish Civil War as a journalist and the Hotel Monteleone is proudly memorialized in his short story "Night Before Battle," which takes place during that war.

During his prolific career, Tennessee Williams produced dozens of plays, poems, and novels. He first visited the Hotel Monteleone as a young child, and always claimed it was his favorite hotel. He was so enamored of it that he included it in his play *The Rose Tattoo*. As a tribute, the Hotel Monteleone is the headquarters of the Tennessee Williams Festival, held in March each year.

Sugar-Free Cheesecakes

*Yields 1 Almond, 1 Lime, and
  1 Chocolate Cheesecake*

Chocolate Bases
1 ½ cups unsalted butter, melted
3 tablespoons cocoa powder
⅓ cup cocoa powder
1 tablespoon vanilla extract

¾ cup all-purpose flour
8 eggs, slightly beaten
3 tablespoons sugar substitute
  (chef prefers Equal)
Cheesecake Filling
3 pounds cream cheese
1 ½ cups sugar substitute
2 tablespoons vanilla extract
1 ¼ cups sour cream
Cheesecake Flavorings
2 tablespoons almond extract
⅓ cup lime juice, to which a few drops of
  green food coloring has been added
½ cup chocolate syrup (3 tablespoons cocoa
  mixed with ⅓ cup water)
Garnishes
Yellow apple slices, tossed with a little
  lemon juice
Red apple slices, tossed with a little
  lemon juice

Chocolate Bases
  Preheat oven to 350 degrees. Lightly butter 3 12-inch springform pans and line with parchment paper.
  Place melted butter in a large mixing bowl.
  Mix together cocoa powder and water. Incorporate into melted butter using a whisk. Add vanilla and mix well. Stir in

Continued next page

flour, eggs and sugar substitute, mixing well after each addition.

Divide batter between prepared springform pans. Bake 8–10 minutes. Cool and reserve.

Cheesecake Filling

Using a large mixer, beat cream cheese until smooth. Add sugar substitute, vanilla, and sour cream. Mix well.

Divide this mixture equally between three mixing bowls. Add almond extract to one, lime juice and food coloring to another, and chocolate to third, stirring each to blend well.

Pour each flavored cheesecake filling into a springform pan holding a cooled chocolate base, and smooth fillings with a small spatula. (At this point you have 3 cheesecakes.)

Bake cheesecakes 15–20 minutes. Remove from oven and let cool 30–60 minutes. Invert cheesecakes onto cardboard discs and remove parchment paper.

To serve, remove cheesecakes from springform pans. Using a knife that has been dipped in hot water, cut small wedges from each cheesecake. Place one of each flavor onto serving plates to form a stack of three. Garnish with fanned apple slices.

PINK MANGO SAUCE

½ pound fresh mangos, peeled and cut into
  ½-inch dice
2 tablespoons sugar (or more to taste)
1 teaspoon fresh lemon juice (optional)

Combine all ingredients in a food processor and blend until smooth. Strain through a fine-meshed sieve and put in a non-aluminum container.

Sauce may be made ahead, refrigerated, then warmed to room temperature for serving.

Use as a garnish for fresh fruits, pound cake, or any dessert that could use some flair.

Bayona

Nestled in a 200-year-old Creole Cottage in the oldest section of the historic French Quarter, Bayona is one of the jewels in the Big Easy's culinary crown. Founded in 1990 by Regina Keever and Chef Susan Spicer, the restaurant was named for Dauphine Street's Spanish name, Camino de Bayona.

Inside you will find three warm elegant dining rooms, a lush and romantic courtyard, an intimate wine room, and Chef Spicer's eclectic global cuisine. Dine at Bayona and immerse yourself in its romantic environment.

Each of the three dining rooms has its own signature: the Bayona Room, with its stained glass accents and picture window; the Dyer Room, with its *trompe l'oeil* depiction of the Mediterranean countryside created by artist Joel Dyer; and the main dining room, which is dominated by elaborate arrangements of flowers.

The patio is open for dining most of the year, weather permitting. It is landscaped with lush tropical greenery, colorful fruit trees, and a gently gurgling fountain, much the same way Creole families maintained their private gardens hundreds of years ago.

The intimate wine room is an additional treasure that is secluded from the bustle of the rest of the dining rooms. It is lined with elegant wine bins and exposed beams. It also serves as a private banquet room.

Defying definition or simple classification, Susan Spicer's food moves across a spectrum of styles and influences with only one unifying thread: top-quality ingredients whose flavors always shine through. You will find hints of the Mediterranean, the Far East, North Africa, France, Italy, and the United States. Chef Spicer refuses to be tied down to a single tradition or genre. For that reason, dining at Bayona is always a unique experience. Reservations required.

Bayona

430 Rue Dauphine

New Orleans, Louisiana 70112

(504) 525-4455

www.bayona.com

GRILLED DUCK BREAST
WITH PEPPER JELLY GLAZE

Serves 8

8 boneless duck breasts (approximately
   6 ounces each), skin on, fat trimmed

2 tablespoons coarse salt

1 teaspoon ground black pepper

1 teaspoon chopped thyme

1 teaspoon chopped rosemary

Mix pepper, thyme, and rosemary together into an herb mixture. Sprinkle salt and herb mixture on the skin of the breasts. Refrigerate for several hours, or let stand about ½ hour before cooking.

Grill or sauté duck skin-side down for about 8 minutes, then turn and cook about 2 more minutes.

Remove from heat, let stand about 2 minutes, then slice into 5–6 pieces, and arrange on plate, skin side up.

Pepper Jelly Glaze

2 tablespoons shallots, chopped

6 ounces sherry vinegar

3 cups flavored broth, made from roasted
   duck bones

3 tablespoons Hot Pepper Jelly

1 fresh jalapeño, seeded and finely minced
   (optional)

2 tablespoons butter

Combine shallots, vinegar, and broth in a small pot and bring to a boil. Reduce heat and simmer until liquid is reduced to about a cup.

Whisk in pepper jelly, then butter. Season to taste with salt, and add more vinegar if sauce is too sweet.

Add jalapeño if desired.

GOAT CHEESE CROUTON
WITH MUSHROOMS IN MADEIRA CREAM

Serves 4

4 slices 7-grain bread, toasted
$1/4$ cup fresh goat cheese, softened
2 tablespoons butter, softened

Mix goat cheese with butter and then spread on toasted bread (about ⅛-inch thick). Trim crust and cut in half. Set aside.

Madeira Cream

2 tablespoons shallots, finely chopped
4 ounces Madeira, medium dry
   (Rainwater or Sercial)
$3/4$ cup whipping cream

In a small pot or saucepan, simmer shallots in Madeira until liquid is reduced by half. Add cream, bring to a boil, then reduce heat and simmer about 5–10 minutes, until cream thickens slightly.

Mushrooms

$1/2$ pound mushrooms (mix of oysters, shiitakes
   or chanterelles)
3 tablespoons butter
$1/2$ teaspoon garlic, minced
Madeira Cream
Salt and pepper
2 teaspoon chives, snipped

Remove tough stems from mushrooms and slice or tear into pieces.

Melt butter in sauté pan and cook mushrooms over medium-high heat until golden brown and slightly crispy. Stir in garlic and Madeira Cream. Turn heat to high and boil for about 2 minutes, or until mushrooms have absorbed most of the cream. Season with salt and pepper and toss in chives.

Place toast with the cheese in a hot oven or broiler just long enough to brown. Remove from the heat, arrange on plates and divide mushrooms equally. Garnish with more chives, if desired.

Galatoire's

Galatoire's

209 Bourbon St

New Orleans, Louisiana 70130

(504) 525-2021

Galatoire's was founded by Jean Galatoire, who came to America from the foothills of the French Pyrenees. In 1880, he opened Galatoire's Restaurant & Guest House Inn in Birmingham, Alabama. He closed the inn and moved to New Orleans in 1900. In 1905, Jean purchased Victor's Restaurant, established in 1830, at 209 Bourbon Street. He later renamed the restaurant "Galatoire's." It is still in the same location today.

Prior to World War I, three of Jean Galatoire's nephews immigrated from Pau, France, to New Orleans. In 1919, brothers Leon, Justin, and Gabriel purchased their uncle's restaurant. The three brothers operated Galatoire's until Rene Galatoire, Leon's son, took over management, followed by Yvonne Wynne, daughter of Justin.

Today, Galatoire's Restaurant is overseen by General Manager Melvin Rodrigue in close conjunction with David Gooch (grandson of Leon), Michele Galatoire (granddaughter of Leon), and Justin Frey (grandson of Justin). Tradition has been maintained with little change through the decades.

One famous story depicts retired U.S. Senator J. Bennett Johnson waiting outside in line for a table. While the senator waited, President Reagan called the restaurant and asked to speak to the senator. After they completed their conversation, Senator Johnson graciously returned *from the phone inside* to his position *outside* in line and waited his turn to be seated. The senator knew that the tradition of "first come, first served" applied to all customers.

Employee loyalty contributes greatly to the success of Galatoire's. While the average employee has been there for ten years, the Executive Chef, Milton Prudence, is a veteran of more than thirty years.

Customer loyalty is also legendary. Marian Atkinson, a cousin of General George S. Patton, dined at Galatoire's regularly from 1916 until her death in 2001. During a twenty-year period, she dined almost every night at the same table, greeting countless patrons.

In 2002, Galatoire's was nominated for the venerable James Beard Foundation's award for the Most Outstanding Restaurant in the Country.

TURTLE SOUP

Serves 8–10

1 cup cooking oil
2 ribs celery, chopped
1 yellow onion, diced
$1/2$ bell pepper, diced
1 pound turtle meat, ground
2 tablespoons paprika
$2/3$ cup flour
5 cups brown stock
1 tomato, crushed
2 tablespoons tomato purée
$1/4$ teaspoon cayenne pepper
1 teaspoon white pepper
1 tablespoon salt
1 teaspoon ground thyme
1 tablespoon minced garlic
Juice of $1/2$ lemon
$1/2$ cup sherry wine
2 hard-boiled eggs, sieved
2 tablespoons parsley, chopped

In a medium-sized pot (5-quart), heat the cooking oil on a medium-high setting. Add the celery, onion, bell pepper, and ground turtle meat. Stir and cook until the vegetables are transparent and turtle meat begins to brown.

Add paprika and flour, then stir to blend evenly. Add the brown stock, constantly stirring until the soup thickens. Add the crushed tomato and tomato purée and stir. Add cayenne and white peppers, salt and thyme. Stir. Add the garlic, the juice of ½ lemon, and sherry wine and continue to stir. Add the sieved hard-boiled eggs and parsley and stir.

TROUT MEUNIÈRE AMANDINE

Serves 6

4 eggs, plus one for egg wash
1 quart whole milk
6 7–8-ounce fillets of speckled trout,
    cleaned and boned
2 cups all-purpose flour
Salt
Black pepper
Oil for frying
3 cups sliced almonds
3 medium lemons
Meunière Butter (recipe follows)

Preheat the oven to 300 degrees. Place the almonds in a pan and roast them for 20–25 minutes, stirring every 5 minutes or so. When they become a light golden brown, remove from the oven and set aside.

Whisk eggs and whole milk and season with salt and pepper. Season the trout fillets with salt and pepper and dust in flour.

Submerge the floured trout in egg wash. Remove fillets from egg wash gently and allow the excess to drip off. Put the filets back into the flour (in the restaurant the saying goes, "flour, wash, flour").

Gently shake off excess flour and fry in oil, heated to 350 degrees, for 4–5 minutes (*Note:* Test the readiness of oil by sprinkling a pinch of flour over it. The flour will brown instantly when the oil is the correct temperature). Remove fish from oil when crust is golden brown.

Top each fried trout fillet with almonds and warmed meunière butter. Garnish with lemon wedges and serve at once.

Meunière Butter

1 pound salted butter
1 tablespoon fresh lemon juice
1 tablespoon red wine vinegar

Melt butter in a medium saucepan over low heat, whisking continuously until the milk fats begin browning and the sauce becomes a dark golden brown. Remove from heat and continue to whisk slowly, adding lemon juice and vinegar to the brown butter. The sauce will begin to froth until the liquids have evaporated. Once the acids have been incorporated and cease to froth, stop whisking and set aside.

CRAB SARDOU

Serves 6

1 cup prepared Hollandaise Sauce
Creamed Spinach (recipe follows)
12 artichokes
2 pounds jumbo lump crabmeat
$1/2$ cup clarified butter

In a large pot, submerge the artichokes in water and boil for approximately 30 minutes, until the stems are tender. Allow the artichokes to cool, and peel the leaves from the hearts. Using a spoon or your thumb, remove and discard the hearts, leaving the bottom of the artichokes.

While waiting for the artichokes to cook and cool, prepare the Creamed Spinach, placing on the side.

Sauté the crabmeat in the clarified butter until hot, being careful not to break the lumps. Remove from heat.

Arrange serving plates and spoon equal portions of the Creamed Spinach onto the plates. Place 2 peeled artichoke bottoms into the bed of spinach. Drain excess butter from the crabmeat and spoon equal portions into the cavities of the bottoms. Finally, top with a generous portion of Hollandaise Sauce.

Creamed Spinach

3 cups cooked spinach
1 cup Bechamel Sauce (recipe follows)
Salt and pepper

In a sauté pan, fold the spinach and bechamel sauce together and simmer over low heat. Salt and pepper to taste.

Bechamel Sauce

$1/4$ cup butter
1 cup of milk
$1/4$ cup of flour

Heat milk until it simmers. Melt the butter and add the flour to make a roux. Continue whisking on low heat to cook the flour but do not allow it to remain on the heat long enough to change from a blonde roux to a brown roux. Add ½ of the heated milk to the roux while constantly whisking. This mixture will become thick like a paste. Add the remaining milk and whisk until smooth.

The Delta Queen

The Delta Queen Steamboat Company can trace its roots to a warm June day in 1890—not in Cincinnati, long the heart of Steamboatin'® in America, nor in New Orleans, long associated with Steamboatin' as its largest Southern port. No, it was in Nashville, Tennessee, on the Cumberland River, where a newly licensed river pilot, Capt. Gordon Christopher Greene, attended an auction to buy a steamboat.

On the advice of a wise old roustabout, he chose the H.K. Bedford and created the Greene Line Steamers for service on the upper Ohio and Kanawha rivers. His young bride, Mary Becker Greene, soon began standing watch in the pilothouse with him and rapidly learned the river. Capt. Mary became one of the first licensed women pilots. The Greene Line expanded as more vessels were added to the fleet, and "home" for the fledgling Greene family was almost always aboard one of their boats.

Capt. Gordon's Greene Line survived many financial, political, and commercial obstacles. After skillfully merging with its rivals, the Greene Line triumphed as more and more steamboats retired from the river. Realizing that freight would not always sustain the line, Capt. Gordon expanded his operations to include passengers. At Capt. Mary's suggestion, he inaugurated a special charter down the Ohio River to the St. Louis World's Fair. It was such a success that he scheduled several more during the fair's duration.

After Capt. Gordon passed away in 1927, his family took over the reins and guided the Greene Line into the stormy days of World War II. With a population starved for affordable wartime getaways on the home front, overnight Steamboatin' vacations aboard the Greene Line vessels became wildly popular. The company steamed out of the war years strong and robust. The family cast around for a new luxury steamboat to augment the often filled-to-capacity Gordon C. Greene—and found it in California!

The river steamers Delta Queen® and Delta King were part of the Navy's large "mothball fleet" near the Sacramento River. Both had served gallantly during the war, functioning as troop carriers or yard ferry boats in San Francisco Bay. The Delta Queen even served as an elegant

The Delta Queen Steamboat Co.

Robin Street Wharf

1380 Port of New Orleans Place

New Orleans, Louisiana 70130

(504) 586-0631

114

hostess for delegates to the United Nations Founding Conference, and at one point, was a floating gun installation that covered famed Alcatraz Penitentiary during a prisoner uprising.

For a bid of slightly more than $47,000, the Greene Line acquired the Delta Queen at government auction. Shortly thereafter, they were offered the Delta King by its bid winner, who had been unaware he was buying a river paddlewheeler instead of an ocean-going freighter. Considering it had cost nearly $1 million to build and outfit each of the sister boats, the Greene Line Steamers had gotten a real bargain.

But the Delta Queen was thousands of miles away from the Mississippi River system. Under the supervision of Capt. Fred Way, a longtime friend of the Greene family, the Delta Queen was boarded up like a giant piano box and towed down the California coast, through the Panama Canal, across the Gulf of Mexico, and up the Mississippi. Under its own power, it steamed proudly upriver to Cincinnati and then to Pittsburgh, where it underwent a thorough refurbishment.

In 1948, the Delta Queen joined the Greene Line's fleet and took her place on the Mississippi system. Capt. Mary Greene, affectionately known to riverfolk as "Ma Greene," moved into a specially outfitted

suite on the cabin deck. She passed away several months later, having served 55 years on the river. Her daughter-in-law, Letha Greene, then took over the company.

An economic downturn in the late '50s threatened the company and Mrs. Greene sold all the vessels in the Greene Line's fleet except for the Delta Queen. Soon it became apparent that she would have to shut down operations entirely.

115

Fortunately, Richard Simonton, a California businessman enamored with his vacations on the Delta Queen, stepped in and rescued the company.

He hired a brilliant young publicist named Betty Blake to help revitalize national interest in paddlewheel vacations on America's heartland rivers. She was so successful that, by the mid-1960s, the Greene Line had paid off its entire debt, including the mortgage on the Delta Queen. But just as things were looking particularly rosy, Congress passed an American version of the international Safety of Life at Sea (SOLAS) convention. The days of wooden passenger vessels were numbered—the Delta Queen, with its rich woodwork, included.

Betty Blake organized a nationwide "Save the Queen" campaign. Petitions flooded the halls of Congress, and she and Steamboatin's many supporters ultimately triumphed. The Delta Queen continues to operate today under a special congressional exception to SOLAS legislation.

Yes, Steamboatin' endures, just as it has through floods, wars, political opposition, and financial challenges. Because of river enthusiasts' affection for this cherished institution, Steamboatin' will always be a fixture on America's heartland rivers. And today's Steamboaters will proudly keep those big red paddlewheels churnin', their wake beating out the rhythm of an American way of life that is kept alive by The Delta Queen, The American Queen, and the Mississippi Queen.

MISSISSIPPI MUD PIE

Serves 6

Chocolate Pecan Brownie

4 ounces unsweetened chocolate

1 cup unsalted butter, softened

$\frac{1}{2}$ teaspoon salt

4 whole eggs

1 teaspoon vanilla extract

2 cups sugar

1 cup flour

1 cup pecan pieces

Melt chocolate and let cool. Whip butter and add sugar and eggs. Mix well. Add melted chocolate and flour and mix well. Fold in pecans.

Pour into greased 8-inch by 11-inch by 2-inch pan and bake at 375 degrees for approximately 30 minutes. Turn out on flat surface and cool.

Coffee Ice Cream

2 cups whole milk

3 cups heavy cream

1$\frac{1}{4}$ cups sugar

4 whole eggs

$\frac{1}{2}$ teaspoon vanilla

$\frac{1}{4}$ cup coffee reduction (4 cups reduced to $\frac{1}{4}$ cup)

Scald milk and cream. Add sugar and dissolve.

In a separate bowl, beat eggs, vanilla, and coffee reduction. Slowly add milk mixture to eggs, whipping continuously.

Return to heat and cook for about 15 minutes over low heat or until mixture coats a spoon. Stir constantly.

Let cool overnight and freeze in ice cream freezer.

Whipped Cream

2 cups heavy whipping cream

1 cup confectionery sugar

2 teaspoons chocolate liquor

Whip together in chilled mixing bowl until stiff. Makes $\frac{3}{4}$ cup.

To prepare Mississippi Mud Pie, top brownie with ice cream and freeze until set. Top with whipping cream and freeze. Cut into 6–8 equal portions and top with warm chocolate syrup. Garnish with pecan pieces.

Steamboat lore holds that chocolate brownies originated on Mississippi River paddlewheelers, so it is fitting that they are part of this recipe. The soil deposited by the Mississippi is some of the richest in the world; this Mississippi Mud Pie is richer still.

Bon Ton Café

Established in 1953 and housed in the historic 1840s Natchez Building, the Bon Ton Café is New Orleans' oldest Cajun restaurant. Carefully presided over by the Pierce family from its beginning, the Bon Ton serves the authentic, more traditional preparations of Cajun cuisine from century-old family recipes created along the bayous of South Louisiana.

Checkered red and white tablecloths, wrought iron chandeliers, and soft brick walls combine with a friendly, experienced staff to create a comfortable but stylish atmosphere and a dining experience that will be fondly remembered. In July of 1998, former President William Jefferson Clinton held a private dinner party at Bon Ton.

Bon Ton Café

401 Magazine

New Orleans, Louisiana 70130

(504) 524-3386

OYSTERS ALVIN

Serves 1

1 dozen oysters (freshly shucked)

2 cups flour

$1/4$ cup margarine

1 teaspoon paprika

1 teaspoon parsley, chopped

$1/2$ cup beef broth (bouillon)

3 cups frying oil

Juice of $1/2$ lemon

Salt to taste ($1/4$ teaspoon)

Pepper to taste ($1/2$ teaspoon)

Dust oysters in flour. Deep-fry in preheated oil (350 degrees) until golden brown. Remove and drain.

Melt margarine in skillet. Add beef broth and simmer until mixture thickens slightly. Place fried oysters in mixture. (The bottoms of the oysters become soaked while the tops remain crisp.) Season with salt, pepper, and lemon and sprinkle lightly with paprika.

Place in broiler until oysters brown slightly. Sprinkle with parsley and serve around bouillon rice, adding sauce from oysters.

EGGPLANT, SHRIMP, AND CRABMEAT ÉTOUFFÉE

Serves 4

4 medium eggplants, peeled and cut into pieces
1 cup yellow onion, chopped
$^1/_2$ cup bell pepper, chopped
$^1/_4$ cup celery, chopped
2 tablespoons celery, chopped
2 tablespoons garlic, chopped
$^1/_2$ cup parsley, chopped
$^1/_4$ pound (1 stick) margarine
1 $^1/_2$ pounds peeled shrimp (90–110)
1 pound fresh picked jumbo lump crabmeat
Salt and pepper to taste

Melt margarine in a medium-sized pot. Add onions, bell pepper, celery, and garlic. Sauté seasonings until cooked limp.

Boil eggplant cubes in a separate pot until cooked. Remove and strain. Add shrimp to pot with seasoning. Heat over low to medium flame and bring to simmer. Add cooked eggplant. Stir shrimp and seasoning and eggplant until evenly combined. Add salt and pepper and mix throughout.

Allow to smother 20 minutes, adding a small amount of water if necessary to keep moist. Taste for seasoning. Add crabmeat and parsley and mix throughout. Remove from heat.

Serve around rice pilaf. Garnish with sprig of parsley.

BOUILLON RICE

1 cup cooked rice (place on side)
1 teaspoon margarine
$^1/_4$ cup beef broth (bouillon)
$^1/_4$ cup mushrooms, chopped
$^1/_4$ cup onions, chopped
$^1/_4$ teaspoon salt
$^1/_4$ teaspoon pepper

Sauté margarine, onions, broth, mushrooms, salt and pepper until onions are clear. Add to cooked rice and stir over low heat until rice absorbs the liquid.

Mound rice onto plate, surround with Oysters Alvin, and serve.

119

Bon Ton Shrimp Remoulade Salad

Serves 8

32 large gulf shrimp, unpeeled

1 package crab boil

2 quarts water

Salt to taste

Romaine lettuce (for 8 salads)

4 ripe tomatoes

Remoulade Sauce

2 cups Creole mustard

2 cups Grey Poupon mustard

4 green onions, chopped with stems

2 cups olive oil

2 tablespoons sugar

1 tablespoon paprika

Pour water and crab boil into pot and add salt and pepper to taste. Bring mixture to a boil and add shrimp. Bring back to a boil and cook 8–10 minutes or until shrimp are cooked.

Strain and allow shrimp to cool. Peel and de-vein shrimp.

Make remoulade sauce by combining both mustards with chopped onions, olive oil, sugar, and paprika. Mix together until blended to smoothness (A small amount of water may have to be added to achieve this).

Place shrimp over bed of chopped lettuce and cover with remoulade sauce. Garnish with fresh tomato wedges.

"New Orleans food is as delicious as the less criminal forms of sin."
Mark Twain

CRABMEAT IMPERIAL

Serves 4

2 pounds fresh picked jumbo lump crabmeat

1 cup green onions, chopped with bulbs and stems

$1/4$ cup pimentos, chopped

1 cup olive oil

$1/2$ cup mushrooms, sliced

$1/2$ cup sherry wine

$1/4$ cup parsley, chopped

Salt to taste

12 toasted bread points—cut French bread in lengths to a point (toast points should be approximately 4 inches in length)

Sauté green onions and mushrooms in 1 cup of olive oil until clear or limp. Add crabmeat, pimento, and sherry and allow to marinate until warm throughout. Season with salt to taste.

Place 3 toast points per serving on plate with wide ends of toast meeting in the middle and points facing out as a star. Mound crabmeat on top of toast. Sprinkle lightly with parsley. Garnish with sprig of parsley.

Fairmont Hotel New Orleans

Fairmont Hotel New Orleans

123 Baronne Street

New Orleans, Louisiana 70112

(504) 529-7111

Much of the allure of the legendary Fairmont Hotel New Orleans lies in its colorful history. Built in 1893 as the fashionable Grunewald, the hotel rose to national fame as the Roosevelt from 1923–1965.

Eight U.S. presidents have stayed under its roof, including Coolidge, Eisenhower, Kennedy, Ford, Bush, and Clinton. Royalty, world leaders, and many of Hollywood's biggest celebrities have called this grand hotel home during their visits to New Orleans. But its most frequent guest was Louisiana's most extraordinary politician, Huey Long, born August 30, 1893, the same year The Grunewald opened its doors.

The Roosevelt Hotel (named for Teddy Roosevelt) and general manager, Seymour Weiss, played an important, on-going role throughout Long's political career during the late '20s to mid-'30s. Son of a merchant in Abbeville, Weiss started work at the Roosevelt in 1925 as manager of the barbershop. He then rapidly rose to general manager, president and principal owner of the hotel. In 1928, then running for governor, Huey Long met Seymour Weiss and chose the Roosevelt as his personal headquarters. The two became friends and Weiss grew to be one of Long's most trusted advisors, as well as his unofficial treasurer for all political and personal operations, working strictly in cash.

Long lived in one of the Roosevelt's finest suites. Popular lore has it that he spent so much time at the hotel, he built a 90-mile highway directly from the state capitol in Baton Rouge to the Roosevelt! Even today, on leaving the Fairmont from the Baronne Street entrance, a right-hand turn puts you on Highway 61 (Airline Drive) straight to Baton Rouge.

One of Long's favorite places to do business in the Roosevelt was the Main Bar, now the Sazerac, home to its namesake cocktail and the Ramos Gin Fizz. Huey and "all the king's men" were ever present in the Main Bar, planning their political strategy. He so liked the Ramos Gin Fizz that he once made headlines in New York by flying bartender Sam Guarino from the Main Bar to a hotel he was visiting there. His sole purpose was to show his Yankee friends how to make the drink.

Huey also spent a lot of time dancing in the Blue Room, the hotel's premier nightclub, which featured the top entertainers of the era. According to Castro Carazo, the Blue Room's orchestra leader, Huey's favorite songs were "Smoke Gets in Your Eyes," That Lonesome Road," and especially "Harvest Moon." Huey invited Carazo to collaborate in writing songs, with Carazo writing the music and Huey the words. Together they wrote Huey's theme song, "Every Man a King."

Several books and movies have been made about Huey Long, all of which include Huey's life and times at the Roosevelt. Many of his most important moments and milestones occurred there and the stories are endless. The friendship between Weiss and Long continued until Long's death. Weiss was at his bedside when Long died from an assassin's bullet in 1935.

The Blue Room was the city's premier supper club, offering fine dining and world-class entertainment. Marlene Dietrich, Jimmy Durante, Tony Bennett, Tina Turner, Frank Sinatra, Sophie Tucker, Joe E. Lewis, and Jimmy Durante all played the room. They were backed by equally big names. These included the big bands

of Glenn Miller, The Dorsey Brothers, Guy Lombardo, and Sammy Kaye.

The Blue Room is located above what was believed to be the first nightclub in America. It was called the Cave, and it opened in 1908, offering lavish revues with Ziegfeld-style chorus girls and live Dixieland bands in a setting of stalactites and waterfalls.

The Fairmont New Orleans was also the model for Arthur Hailey's novel *Hotel,* with some characters based on staff members.

Today, the Fairmont New Orleans remains one of the city's most colorful treasures.

123

PROSCIUTTO-WRAPPED GULF MAHI MAHI FILLET
WITH CREMINI MUSHROOM AND POTATO RISOTTO

Serves 6

6 portions of 6-ounce cleaned Mahi Mahi fillets
6 ounces very thinly sliced prosciutto ham
1 pound fresh Cremini mushrooms, quartered
1 pound small yellow potato, diced
4 ounces sliced smoked bacon
4 ounces shallots, finely diced
1 ounce garlic, finely diced
2 cups veal or chicken stock
4 ounces heavy cream
2 ounces extra-virgin olive oil
2 ounces unsalted butter
4 ounces freshly shaved Reggiano Parmesan cheese
Freshly chopped chervil
Splash of truffle oil
Salt and freshly cracked black pepper
Dried prosciutto straws (see below)
Fresh tarragon or other herb for plate decoration

Season the mahi mahi fillets with salt and pepper. Wrap the fillets completely in the prosciutto ham and secure with toothpicks.

Heat half of the olive oil in a heavy-bottomed skillet and sear the fillets in the olive oil on all sides. Finish baking in a preheated oven at 375 degrees until cooked (about 10–12 minutes). Remove from oven and keep warm.

Heat the remaining olive oil in a sauté pan until very hot and toss the mushrooms quickly until slightly cooked. Remove from pan and set aside.

In the same pan add the bacon, butter, shallots, and garlic and sweat for a few minutes. Add all the potatoes and mix well. Add the chicken stock and the cream, and simmer over low-medium heat for about 20 minutes, being careful not to overcook the potatoes. Add to this mixture the reserved mushrooms and cook briefly. Add the fresh chopped chervil and check the seasoning.

Spoon the mixture (not too thick) on the bottom of a large plate. Place the Mahi Mahi fillet on top of the risotto. Garnish with the shaved Parmesan cheese, fresh herbs, and dried prosciutto straws. Lightly drizzle with truffle oil for intense flavor.

Note: Dried prosciutto straws are made by tightly rolling long, thinly sliced prosciutto into the shape of a drinking straw and drying in a 150-degree oven for about 1½–2 hours.

> *"Fish, to taste right must swim three times—*
> *in water, in butter and in wine."*
> Polish proverb

REDFISH AND SHRIMP CHUPE
WITH FRESH CORN AND CILANTRO

Serves 4

4 ounces onions, diced small

4 ounces leeks, diced small

6 ounces fresh tomato, diced small

4 ounces green pepper, diced small

1 ounce garlic, finely chopped

2 ounces extra-virgin olive oil

1 pound potatoes, diced

4 ounces carrot, diced small

8 ounces fresh corn kernels (or frozen if fresh
   cannot be obtained)

2 quarts light fish stock (or chicken stock)

4 ounces heavy cream

4 egg yolks, hard boiled and chunked

2 fresh limes cut for juice

8 ounces redfish fillet, cut into $1/2$-inch cubes

8 ounces shrimp, peeled and de-veined

Freshly chopped cilantro

Salt and freshly cracked black pepper

Abundant vegetable oil for frying

All-purpose flour for seafood coating

In a deep pan, sweat the onions, leeks, tomato, peppers, and garlic in the olive oil until well cooked. Add the diced potatoes, carrots, and corn and continue to cook for another 5 minutes. Add the fish stock and cook for about 45 minutes or so until the soup comes together and starts to thicken slightly (some of the potatoes may fall apart but this is OK). Add the cream and chopped cilantro. Season with salt and pepper and boil one last time, then squeeze fresh lime juice to taste.

In another bowl, season the redfish and shrimp with salt and pepper and coat in flour. Fry in abundant vegetable oil until golden brown and cooked through. Remove from oil and dry on paper towels.

Ladle soup into large deep soup plate. Top with browned cubes of fish and shrimp and crumbled egg yolk and garnish with fresh sprig of cilantro. Serve immediately piping hot with your favorite hot sauce!

Mulate's

The nineteenth-century building housing Mulate's of New Orleans is a fine example of masonry architecture. According to rumor, it was originally built as a hotel and was subsequently used as a stable for the Faubacher Brewery, a cotton warehouse, and an icehouse.

Located in the bustling warehouse district, the building has been transformed into an authentic Cajun dancehall which offers the sights and sounds of the bayou in the heart of the city. Mulate's is recognized throughout the world as the King of Cajun dine-and-dance halls. It features live Cajun music and dancing along with great authentic Cajun food, seven days a week. The restaurant even has its beer, whose label proudly boasts that it is "Brewed to the Cajun Taste."

Just what is a Cajun? The word Cajun refers to French people from southern Louisiana. They are also called Acadians because their ancestors were from Canada. Acadians were French settlers who dominated the area now known as Nova Scotia in the 1600s. In the mid-1700s, they were forced out by the British. Thousands of these exiled Acadians moved to south Louisiana, following the French pioneers that had preceded them there.

Eventually Acadian culture came to dominate south Louisiana. The name "Cajun" is a variation of "Acadian," but it represents the old world French culture of Louisiana, combined to a lesser degree with other European cultures imported by German, English, and Spanish immigrants, as well as local Indians.

Mulate's is a place where Cajuns come to celebrate their heritage and the world comes to join them in their celebrations. It has been named as one of the most underrated restaurants in the US by *The Wall Street Journal*.

Mulate's

201 Julia Street

New Orleans, Louisiana 70130

(504) 522-1492

(800) 854-9149

www.mulates.com

CRABMEAT STUFFING

Serves 4

3/4 cup butter or margarine

2 medium bell peppers, chopped

3 large onions, chopped

3 stalks celery, chopped

1 teaspoon salt

1 teaspoon cayenne pepper

2 cups bread crumbs

1 tablespoon flour

3 eggs

1 handful parsley, chopped

3/4–1 pound claw crabmeat, shells removed

Melt butter or margarine. Sauté vegetables on medium heat until translucent (approximately 15 minutes). Season with salt and cayenne pepper.

Combine all remaining ingredients except for crabmeat. Add sautéed vegetable mixture and mix well. Fold in crabmeat.

To Fry: Batter in egg mixture. Cover with bread crumbs. Fry until golden brown.

To Bake: Heat oven to 350 degrees. Batter in egg mixture. Cover with bread crumbs. Bake approximately 20–30 minutes.

You can stuff fish, chicken, or turkey or fry it alone.

CRAWFISH ÉTOUFFÉE

Serves 4

1 1/4 stick butter or margarine

1 medium onion, diced

2 stalks celery, diced

1 small bell pepper, diced

1 pound peeled crawfish tails

1/2 teaspoon salt

1/2 teaspoon cayenne pepper

2 cups cooked white rice

For garnish:

1/2 cup chopped parsley

2 green onions, chopped

Melt butter or margarine. Add diced onions, celery, and bell pepper. Sauté on medium heat until vegetables are translucent, approximately 15 minutes.

Add crawfish, salt, and cayenne pepper. Stir well. Cook covered on low heat for approximately 15 minutes.

Add chopped parsley or green onions just before serving if desired. Serve over white rice.

Variation: Add 1 can cream of mushroom soup just before adding the crawfish.

127

Emeril's Delmonico

One of Emeril's newest establishments isn't really new at all. Delmonico, an icon in the New Orleans restaurant industry, has been in business since 1895 and closed its doors in February 1997 to re-establish ownership.

The original Delmonico began in 1827 as a small café and pastry shop on William Street in what is now the Financial District in lower Manhattan, New York City. After expanding next door in 1830, it became the first restaurant or public dining room in the United States. Destroyed in 1835 by the Great Fire, it reopened nearby in an opulent setting built exclusively for Delmonico. Many classic American dishes are said to have been created at Delmonico, including Lobster Newburg, Chicken à la King, Eggs Benedict, and Baked Alaska.

Anthony Commander, a New Orleans saloon owner himself, was the younger brother of Emile Commander, creator of the New Orleans saloon Commander's Palace. Anthony received permission from the New York family to open an independent Delmonico in the Crescent City, and it flourished. The first Delmonico in New York was eventually forced to close in 1923, due to the decline in business associated with Prohibition.

Delmonico first opened in a one-story building that had served as a dairy creamery for five years. A second floor was added later to serve as a gymnasium where patrons could work off the lunch specials. When the restaurant was sold to Anthony LaFranca, he converted the upstairs to a residence for his family. After he passed away in 1943, his widow ran the restaurant for many years until her death in 1975. Her two daughters continued to operate Delmonico until 1997, when it was closed and sold to Chef Emeril Lagasse.

Emeril's Delmonico re-opened its doors in May of 1998 after undergoing an extensive historic renovation. Emeril now brings the high standards of service and cuisine he has established at his three succeeding restaurants to this reinvigorated classic dining establishment. Located on the streetcar line of New Orleans' famed St. Charles Avenue, Emeril's Delmonico offers classic Creole dining. Emeril's Delmonico's ambience and decor match its menu's elegance and sophistication.

Emeril's Delmonico

1300 St. Charles

New Orleans, Louisiana 70130

(504) 525-4937

www.emerils.com

The style of cuisine at Emeril's Delmonico is classic New Orleans Creole reinvented for the contemporary palate. Under its new direction, the restaurant will keep many of the classic items from its former menu while adding the inventive flavors that Chef Emeril Lagasse is known for.

The menu also features prime steaks dry-aged in-house. Tableside service and preparation are in keeping with the classic style of Creole cuisine.

CRABMEAT REMICK

Serves 6

1 ½ teaspoons unsalted butter

1 cup mayonnaise

½ cup chili sauce

2 tablespoons green onions, finely chopped

1 tablespoon fresh lemon juice

1 teaspoon garlic, minced

1 teaspoon dry mustard

1 teaspoon tarragon vinegar

1 teaspoon paprika

1 teaspoon hot sauce

1 pound lump crabmeat, picked over for shells and cartilage

6 ounces (7 strips) bacon, crisply fried and crumbled

6 tablespoons freshly grated Parmigiano-Reggiano

Croutons or toast points

Preheat the oven to 400 degrees. Grease 6 4-ounce ramekins with the butter, place on a baking sheet, and set aside.

Combine the mayonnaise, chili sauce, green onions, lemon juice, garlic, mustard, vinegar, paprika, and hot sauce in a large bowl and mix well. Fold in the crabmeat and mix until well coated with the sauce, being careful not to break up the lumps.

Divide the mixture among the prepared dishes and top each portion with 1 tablespoon each of the bacon and cheese.

Bake until the crabmeat is hot and the cheese is golden brown on top, 8–10 minutes.

Carefully transfer the ramekins to six plates and serve immediately with croutons on the side.

Crabmeat Remick has been a New Orleans menu standard since the 1920s, when it first appeared on the menu at the Pontchartrain Hotel's Caribbean Room, another fine establishment down the street from Delmonico on St. Charles Avenue.

Crabmeat Remick is such a local classic that I put it on the menu when we reopened Delmonico in 1998. It can be made several hours ahead, refrigerated, and then baked just before serving.

FRIED SOFT-SHELLED CRABS AMANDINE

The blue crabs native to the Gulf South and Atlantic coastline shed their hard shells many times as they grow. Before molting, the crabs form a soft new shell under the old one, which hardens within twelve hours. The crabs caught in this soft-shelled state are a popular delicacy in south Louisiana.

When the LaFranca family operated the restaurant, the menu often offered soft-shelled crabs broiled, fried, or stuffed, and served with lemon butter sauce or Creole meunière sauce. The classic French beurre meunière sauce is made by browning butter to a light hazelnut color and then adding lemon juice and parsley. Many New Orleans restaurants have their own particular version. Some meunière sauces are made by combining a rich brown stock with butter, lemon juice, Worcestershire Sauce, and minced parsley. The LaFranca version was simple—their regular lemon butter sauce was cooked just a bit longer to give it a richer color and deeper flavor.

Serves 4

4 jumbo soft-shelled crabs (about 8 ounces each)
1 cup all-purpose flour
1 teaspoon salt
$^1/_4$ teaspoon cayenne
1 cup buttermilk
2 large eggs
1 cup cracker meal
$^1/_3$ cup vegetable oil
12 tablespoons (1 $^1/_2$ sticks) unsalted butter
$^1/_2$ cup sliced almonds, blanched

2 tablespoons fresh lemon juice
1 $^1/_2$ tablespoons Worcestershire
Pinch of salt

Using kitchen shears, cut each crab across the face to remove the eye sockets and the lower mouth. Carefully lift up the apron and remove the gills. Gently rinse under cold running water, pat dry, and set aside.

Combine the flour with the salt and cayenne in a shallow bowl. Whisk together the buttermilk and eggs in another shallow bowl. Put the cracker meal in a third bowl.

Heat enough oil to come to $^1/_2$ inch up the sides of a large cast-iron skillet or Dutch oven over medium-high heat until hot but not smoking.

Dredge crabs in the seasoned flour and dip in the buttermilk mixture, allowing any excess to drip off. Dredge crabs in cracker meal, making sure that the legs are well-breaded.

In two batches, add the crabs to the pan, top-side down, and cook until golden brown and just cooked through, about 2 minutes per side. Drain on paper towels.

Continued next page

130

"*For my part, I travel not to go anywhere, but to go.
I travel for travel's sake. The great affair is to move.*"
Robert Louis Stevenson

Pour the fat from the pan and wipe clean with paper towels. Return the pan to medium heat and add the butter. When the butter begins to foam, add the almonds and cook, stirring, until fragrant and beginning to brown, about 1 minute.

Remove the almonds with a slotted spoon, reduce the heat to low, and cook the butter until it begins to brown and smell nutty, about 1 minute.

Remove from the heat, add the lemon juice, Worcestershire, and salt and stir to combine. Return the pan to low heat and cook until the butter is browned, about 30 seconds.

Remove from heat, add almonds, and swirl to coat with sauce.

To serve, place one crab in the center of each of four large plates. Spoon sauce over crabs and serve immediately.

Le Pavillon Hotel

Le Pavillon Hotel

833 Poydras

New Orleans, Louisiana 70112

(504) 581-3111

Original construction on the 10-story Le Pavillon Hotel, located on Poydras at Baronne, began in 1905. The property was turned over to Mr. Justin Denechaud in 1907 and was known as Hotel Denechaud until 1913, when new owners renamed it the De Soto Hotel. The property quickly became a luxury hot spot, and numerous dignitaries entered the hotel for grand balls and political purposes, as well as for the grandeur and privacy always offered at Le Pavillon.

Records indicate that, during the years of Prohibition, an underground tunnel led from the hotel to a building a block and a half away, evidently "in case of emergencies"—and for discreet VIP passage. The penthouse suite was the original home of the first radio station in the city, WDSU, from 1928–1948. New owners acquired the hotel in the early 1970s and named the hotel Le Pavillon. The French name seemed befitting, as the land was purchased from France more than 200 years ago from Jean Bienville, founder of New Orleans.

The new owner focused on developing Le Pavillon into an outstanding showplace for the city. The search began in Europe, yielding many of the furnishings gracing the halls today, including the massive exterior columns and oversized sculptures carved by Italian artisans to the owner's specifications. The lobby's 11 glistening crystal chandeliers and matching sconces were purchased in Czechoslovakia. The various paintings and furnishings, such as the marble railings, came from the lobby of the Grand Hotel in Paris.

Le Pavillon has become well known for the nightly complimentary snack of peanut-butter-and-jelly sandwiches served with cold milk or hot chocolate in the grand lobby.

Chicken and Shrimp Gumbo

Serves 12

1 medium onion, chopped

1 cup celery, diced

1 cup green bell pepper, diced

1 whole head of garlic, minced

2 cups cut okra

3 cups peeled shrimp, save shells (Cook shells in 3 cups water for 10 minutes, strain, and save)

2 cups chicken, cut up (Roast whole chicken in oven, pull meat from bones, and cook bones in water to cover for 30 minutes to make stock. Strain and save.)

1 ½ cups peanut oil

1 ½ cups flour

Cajun seasoning to taste

Combine oil and flour in a thick soup pot over medium heat. Cook the mixture, stirring continuously until creamy dark brown. Add onion, pepper, and celery. Stir and cook for 5 minutes.

Add garlic and cut okra and both shrimp and chicken stocks to just cover the mixture in the pot. Cook for 30 minutes.

Add shrimp and cooked chicken. Season to taste and cook for 10 minutes over medium heat.

Serve with rice.

Tenderloin of Beef a La Cruz

Serves 2

2 3-ounce filets of beef (high grade)

2–4 ounces jumbo lump crabmeat

3 ounces dried wild mushrooms

4 teaspoons butter

4 teaspoons extra-virgin olive oil

¼ cup flour

Salt and red pepper flakes to taste

1 cup heavy cream

⅓ cup green onion tops, thinly sliced

2 teaspoons fresh basil, cut into ribbons

⅓ cup diced tomatoes (optional)

Soak dried wild mushrooms in a little warm brandy or red wine, then slice thinly.

Combine olive oil and butter in hot skillet.

Season filet medallions and lightly coat in flour. Place in hot skillet and cook on each side until golden brown.

Add mushrooms and some liquor from the mushrooms to skillet. Add cream and reduce until slightly thickened.

Remove filets.

Combine crabmeat, green onions, and tomato and serve over filet.

Garnish with basil and tomatoes.

133

Commander's Palace

Nestled in the middle of the Garden District stands a turquoise and white Victorian fantasy of a building, complete with turrets, columns, and gingerbread. Since 1880, Commander's Palace has been a New Orleans landmark known for the award winning quality of its food and many commodious dining rooms.

The history of this famous restaurant offers a glimpse into New Orleans' antebellum past. In the early 1880s, when Louisiana officially joined the nation, eager young Anglo-Saxons flocked to this promising territory to make their fortunes. Since the Vieux Carré was the stronghold of the proud Creoles, these "Americans" (as they were defined by the Creoles)

Commander's Palace
1403 Washington Avenue
New Orleans, Louisiana 70130
(504) 899-8221

sought a residential section of their own. Thus was born the Garden District, with its stately Greek revival homes and quiet, tree-lined streets.

Here in the Garden District, George W. Cable entertained Mark Twain; here Jefferson Davis spent his last days. And here, in 1880, Emile Commander established the only restaurant patronized by the distinguished neighborhood families. He chose the corner of Washington Avenue and Coliseum Street, a site that had been, in turn, part of the J.F.E. Livaudais Plantation and the faubourg of Lafayette. In 1854 it was engulfed by the city of New Orleans and by 1900, Commander's Palace was attracting gourmets from all over the world.

Under different management in the twenties, its reputation was somewhat spicier. Riverboat captains frequented it and sporting gentlemen met with beautiful women for a rendezvous in the private dining room upstairs. Downstairs, however, the main dining room (with its separate entrance) was maintained in impeccable

respectability for family meals after church and family gatherings of all sorts.

In 1944, Frank and Elinor Moran bought Commander's Palace, refurbished it, and carried on its tradition of excellence with an expanded menu including many recipes still used. When Ella, Dottie, Dick, and John Brennan took over personal supervision of the restaurant in 1974, they began to give the splendid old landmark a new look. It was decided to design rooms and settings indoors which complemented and enhanced the lovely outdoor setting in order to achieve a bright, casual airiness. Walls were torn out and replaced with walls of glass, trellises were handmade for the Garden Room and paintings were commissioned for each room to complement and accent its particular color and design.

Particular attention was paid to the heart and soul of the restaurant: the kitchen and the dishes created there. Commander's cuisine reflects the best of the city—both Creole and American heritages—as well as dishes of Commander's own creating.

135

TURTLE SOUP

If we took a poll and asked New Orleanians what single dish they most associate with Commander's Palace, I am sure it would be Turtle Soup. Recently a gentleman diner told me he had a hard time finding Commander's—he said he hadn't been to New Orleans in 30 years, and we had gone and built an interstate highway which confused him. He then asked if we still had the Turtle Soup he remembered. "Yes sir," I was happy to reply. Funny thing is, our family didn't even own the restaurant 30 years ago.

Serves 5

¾ cup butter
2 ½ pounds turtle meat, medium diced
2 medium onions, medium diced
6 stalks celery, medium diced
30 cloves garlic, minced
3 bell peppers, medium diced
1 tablespoon dried thyme, ground
1 tablespoon dried oregano, ground
4 bay leaves
2 quarts veal stock
1 cup flour
26 ounces dry sherry (750 ml bottle)
1 tablespoon hot sauce
¼ cup Worcestershire sauce
2 large lemons, juiced
3 cups concassée tomatoes
10 ounces fresh spinach, stems removed, washed 3 times, roughly chopped
6 medium eggs, hard-boiled and chopped into large pieces
Salt and freshly cracked pepper to taste

In a large soup pot over medium to high heat, melt ¼ cup butter and brown turtle meat. Season. Cook for about 18–20 minutes or until liquid is almost dry.

Add onions, celery, garlic, and peppers, constantly stirring. Add thyme, oregano, and bay leaves and sauté for about 22 minutes.

Add stock, bring to a boil, and simmer for 30 minutes. Skim any fat that comes to top.

While stock is simmering, make roux. In a small saucepan, melt remaining butter over medium heat. Slowly add flour, a little at a time, constantly stirring with a wooden spoon. Be careful not to burn. After all of the flour has been added, cook (for about 3 minutes) until roux smells nutty, is pale in color, and has the consistency of wet sand. Set aside until soup is ready.

Using a whisk, stir roux into stock mixture vigorously, a little at a time, to prevent lumping. Simmer for about 25 minutes. Stir to prevent sticking on bottom. Add sherry. Bring to a boil. Add hot sauce and Worcestershire sauce. Simmer and skim any fat or foam that comes to top. Add lemon juice and tomatoes. Bring back to simmer. Add spinach and egg. Bring to simmer and adjust seasoning.

Chef's Notes: This is like a stew, eaten as a main dish. We use alligator snapping turtles, which are a farm-raised fresh water species available all year long. Turtle meat usually comes in 2½-pound portions. This soup freezes well.

GUMBO YA-YA

Makes one gallon

1 2 ½-pound chicken, quartered

Salt and pepper to taste

Flour for dusting

¾ cup vegetable oil (any oil with a high smoking point)

¾ cup flour, sifted

3 large onions, medium diced

7 stalks celery, cleaned, medium diced

4 bell peppers, medium diced

12 garlic cloves, minced

1 teaspoon cayenne pepper or to taste

Pinch of dried oregano

Pinch of dried basil

Pinch of dried thyme

4 medium bay leaves

2 ½ quarts cold water

1 ½ pounds Andouille sausage, sliced ¼-inch thick

1 tablespoon filé powder

1 tablespoon hot sauce or to taste

4 cups cooked rice

3 green onions, thinly sliced

Season chicken and dust with flour. Shake off excess flour.

Place oil in a large heavy dry pot and heat oil over high heat until it reaches smoking point, about 3 minutes. Sear chicken until golden brown, about 5 minutes on first side and 4 minutes on second side. Remove from pot.

When oil has returned to smoking point, make a roux by slowly adding flour, stirring constantly with a wooden spoon, until the roux is the color of milk chocolate, about 3–5 minutes. Scraping the sides and bottom of pot while stirring constantly is the key to a good roux. Be careful not to burn it, because you will need to start over if it does burn. When roux has reached desired color, add onions and cook for 1 minute.

Add celery, and cook for 30 seconds.

Add bell peppers, scrape the bottom of the pot, and cook for 1 minute.

Add garlic, cayenne, oregano, basil, thyme, bay leaves, and season to taste. Slowly add the water, stirring constantly to avoid lumps of roux.

Add chicken and sausage. Stir. Bring to a boil. Simmer for about 2½ hours, skimming excess fat from top of gumbo.

When meat falls off bones, remove bones from pot. Adjust to desired consistency by adding water if needed or reducing. Return to a boil and stir in filé. Stir vigorously to avoid clumping until filé is dissolved. Adjust salt and pepper and finish with hot sauce to taste.

Serve over cooked rice and garnish with green onions.

Chef's Notes: Skimming the excess fat from the gumbo is important. Oil is released from the roux and the sausage. Adjust gumbo to desired consistency. Some people like a thick gumbo; others like it thin. For me, it depends on the weather: I like it thick in the colder weather and thinner in the warmer months.

137

The Windsor Court Hotel

A haven for the discriminating traveler, the Windsor Court Hotel offers a touch of England in the heart of New Orleans. The hotel is a favorite among visiting celebrities, including Kevin Costner, Rod Stewart, Luciano Pavarotti, Paul McCartney, Uma Thurman, Prince Albert of Monaco, and President George W. Bush.

The Windsor Court is an expression of all things English. Opened in February 1984 with Princess Anne presiding over the festivities, the hotel stands alone in its British ambiance in a city steeped in French and Spanish history.

Whether visitors are drawn by food, jazz, history, architecture, the sultry sensuality, or the laissez-faire way of New Orleans, travelers choose the Windsor Court for the luxury and level of service that creates memories of indulgence and pampering.

The hotel's location in the heart of the business district provides a dignified respite, yet it is within easy access of the French Quarter, the jazz clubs and restaurants of Bourbon Street, and the antique shops and art galleries of Royal Street. Hotel views to the south capture the Mississippi River, while just blocks west is the emerging Arts District, followed by the antebellum architecture of the Garden District. In addition, the New Orleans Convention Center, Aquarium of the Americas, National D-Day Museum, The Ogden Museum of Southern Art, and the docks for the legendary paddle wheeler tours are all within a 15-minute walk.

Designed to replicate the interior of a stately English manor, the hotel features antiques and period reproductions from the seventeenth and eighteenth centuries. Decorated in soft, restful colors, the lobby and Le Salon are tastefully furnished. High ceilings, intricate moldings, rich woods, beautiful marble, and woven floor coverings add to the evocation of tradition and a civilized upper-class way of life. Original art works provide focal points in every room. Many of the pieces are of British origin, with an emphasis on works that depict the Windsor Castle and life of British royalty. The collection has an estimated value of more than $8 million and includes original works by Reynolds, Gainsborough, and Huysman.

The Windsor Court Hotel

300 Gravier Street

New Orleans, Louisiana 70130

(504) 523-6000

(800) 262-2662

www.windsortcourthotel.com

The hotel is a 23-story, rose-colored granite structure with bronze-tinted, tempered glass. The top two levels are recessed, creating roof-level terraces. The balconies and bay windows project in relief, following the hotel's hexagonal architectural motif. The main entrance opens onto a large, lushly foliaged, brick courtyard with a sparkling fountain. Featured in the center is a John W. Mills sculpture of the dragon-slayer St. George, the medieval symbol of chivalry and valor.

Le Salon is located in the lobby on the first floor. Furnished with plush armchairs and sofas and accented with stunning artwork, this room is known for its soothing quality. Afternoon tea in the British fashion—accompanied by live chamber music—is served daily. By night, Le Salon is New Orleans' first non-smoking lounge, featuring some of the hottest New Orleans jazz musicians, fabulous cocktails (including nearly a dozen different champagne cocktails), and Le Salon's signature tiered appetizer towers, which allow guests to select from a mélange of specialties prepared by Executive Chef Jonathan Wright.

 Ranked as one of *Zagat's* Top Ten Restaurants, The New Orleans Grill (formerly The Grill Room) provides an elegant setting featuring fine furnishings and a warm palate of gold, coral, and cinnamon. The aural setting features jazz, New Orleans blues, and instrumentals inspired by the great crooners. Chef Wright's contemporary European cuisine draws on his French training and the bounty of Louisiana products available.

Fricassee of Chicken
with New Potatoes, Spring Onions, and Morels

Serves 4

8 thighs of free range or organic chicken, or a combination of legs and thighs

24 baby onions or shallots, peeled and left whole

1 cup dried morels, placed in chicken stock until softened

8 ounces baby leeks or spring onions

12 cloves garlic, peeled and left whole

3 1/2 ounces white wine (Riesling would work well)

12 ounces chicken stock (homemade or a brought product)

12 ounces heavy cream

1 dessert spoon full tarragon, chopped

1 dessert spoon full chives, chopped

1 dessert spoon full parsley, chopped

3 dessert spoons Dijon mustard

1 pound fingerling potatoes, peeled and sliced 1/2-inch thick

1 ounce smoked bacon, diced

Place fresh butter in a heavy-bottomed cast iron pan over medium heat. When it begins to foam and turn nut brown, add the chicken pieces. Turn the heat to low and brown (caramelize) evenly all the way around. This will not, as popularly believed, seal in juices, but the caramelizing of the meat gives a wonderful flavor and color.

When caramelized, place the meat in the slow cooker or crock-pot.

Add the wine and chicken stocks to the pan. With a spatula, scrape up the caramelized glaze in the bottom of the pan. Simmer until liquid is reduced by half. Add the cream, bring to a boil, add mustard, season lightly, and whisk to emulsify.

Quickly sauté the morels in a little butter for one minute. This makes a big difference to their flavor. For a real treat, a few drops of grappa can be used to deglaze the morels.

Scatter all the vegetables around the meat in the slow cooker, and then add the sauce. Prepare this at night and allow it to cook slowly through the night or place the dish in the refrigerator until the following morning. Then, turn the slow cooker on low, set the timer for 4 hours (or 3½ hours with the slow cooker on medium). The juice at this point can be reduced and thickened if necessary with a little cornstarch solution.

At the last minute, add the fresh herbs so that their flavors are infused and fresh. This dish is well suited to fresh pasta and sautéed spinach.

SLOW-COOKED LAMB SHANKS, CARROTS, TURNIPS, AND SHALLOTS

Serves 4

4 10–12 ounce lamb shanks (shoulders are better than legs)

8 large shallots, peeled, trimmed, and left whole

12 medium-sized carrots, peeled and trimmed

8 golf ball-sized baby turnips, peeled and trimmed

2 ounces fresh butter

2 ounces olive oil

8 cloves of elephant garlic, peeled and blanched in cold water (bring up to a boil twice)

1 celery heart

1 bouquet Garni (2 sprigs thyme, 1 bay leaf, 1 stem rosemary)

1 pint chicken stock or water

1 pound mixture of above vegetables, 1-inch dice

$\frac{1}{2}$ pint white wine, reduced by $\frac{1}{3}$

Worcestershire sauce

Fresh rosemary or thyme

Place olive oil and fresh butter in a heavy-bottomed cast iron pan over medium heat. When it begins to foam and turn nut brown, add the lamb shanks. Remove any excess fat from the shanks, turn the heat to moderate and brown (caramelize) evenly all the way around.

When caramelized, place the meat in a slow cooker or crock-pot. Pour off excess fat.

Add the wine and chicken stock or water to the pan and, with a spatula, remove the caramelized glaze that has covered the surface. This contains wonderful flavor and color. Reduce by one-third.

Dice the celery and garlic and in a separate pan, caramelize these vegetables. Scatter the cooked diced vegetables around the meat in the slow cooker, and then add the sauce. Add the bouquet Garni, Worcestershire sauce, black pepper, and a little salt. Turn the slow cooker on low and set the timer for 6 hours.

When finished cooking, remove meat carefully from the pot and place on the side. Strain out the vegetables and herbs so you are left with the stock. Pour the diced vegetables and herbs into a pot, add the other whole vegetables, and slowly simmer until they are cooked to your liking. The juice at this point can be reduced and thickened if necessary with a little cornstarch solution.

Place the meat back into the crock-pot. Add vegetables and sauce so that it glazes the meat. At the last minute, add the fresh herbs and serve.

141

BEYOND NEW ORLEANS

Most Louisiana visitors head straight for New Orleans. While there is much to see and do in the city where jazz was born, Louisiana offers an amazing spectrum of diverse landscapes and cultures.

The history of Louisiana truly comes to life in Plantation Country. Wind your way along the Great River Road as you travel back to the 1800s. Throughout this area are many plantations, including the Myrtles, "the most haunted house in America."

Nestled in the center of the state is the capital, Baton Rouge, with its Art Deco-style capitol building, the tallest in the nation. In nearby Cajun Country, you'll discover crawfish étouffée and dance to Zydeco music. Along the Cajun Coast, you can venture into the swamps to see snowy egrets, blue herons, and moss-covered cypress trees or into the warm Gulf of Mexico for a deep-sea fishing excursion.

In the 800,000-acre Kisatchie National Forest of the Crossroads, you might encounter bears, possums, and deer, but you'll rarely see another group of hikers. On the old King's Highway, you'll find the breathtaking Toledo Bend Reservoir, which boasts some of the best fishing, hunting, canoeing, and birding in the country.

Northern Louisiana is a Sportsman's Paradise. Thick, piney woods flourish with wildlife, and clear, sparkling lakes are stocked abundantly with bass and trout.

See all of Louisiana. You won't be disappointed.

Nottoway Plantation

Nottoway Plantation
  Restaurant and Inn
LA Hwy 1
White Castle, Louisiana 70788
(225) 545-2730 or
(866) 4-A-Visit
www.nottoway.com

John Hampden Randolph planned and built Nottoway in 1859, creating a thriving sugarcane business that covered more than 7,000 acres. But it was his wife Emily Jane who saved Nottoway from destruction.

Emily Jane Liddell Randolph was a mother of ten when the Civil War erupted. In 1862, Randolph took his slaves to Texas to work a cotton plantation in order to avoid debt. The Randolphs sent their teenage daughters away to safer territory, and Mrs. Randolph remained on the plantation with the younger children, two visiting lady friends, and a few of her slaves. One of her daughters, Cornelia, kept a diary. It is from this diary, as well as from preserved letters and documents, that we know of Emily Jane's courage.

At one point in 1862, when she was 45 years old, Emily faced down the Union Navy. Gunboats were sailing by the house, and union troops had begun to bivouac on the lawn. Armed with only a dagger, which she tucked into her belt, she went out on the front gallery. She was determined not to let the Union troops into her house.

Many houses along the river had been abandoned. These deserted houses, if not burned, were destroyed by looting and vandalism. As she stood on the front gallery, a group of Confederate soldiers opened fire on the Union troops. The gunboats on the river returned the fire. Though they were not aiming at the house, much of the fire hit it or landed on the grounds.

When the firing became heavy, Emily Jane gathered her children, friends, and slaves and took them all to the ground floor, where the walls were four feet thick. When the barrage was over, she alone had the courage to mount the stairs and assess the damage.

It was in that same year that Emily Jane gave birth to her eleventh and last child, Julia Marceline. Although the Union army camped out several times on the lawn in the course of the war, they never entered the house except to search for weapons. Nottoway served as inspiration for the filming of the movie *Gone with the Wind*. Scarlett O'Hara fashioned her dress from drapes very similar to those seen hanging in the Randolph study.

Today, tourists and/or overnight guests can tour the house, dine in the restaurant, relax on the grounds, or swim in the pool.

"Beat the Summertime Blues" Pasta Salad

Serves 8

1 cup low-fat mayonnaise

1 cup Johnny Jambalaya's Herb Dressing

12 ounces elbow macaroni, cooked and cooled

2 cucumbers, peeled and sliced

2 large Creole tomatoes, quartered and sliced

3 ribs of celery, chopped

1 Vidalia onion, chopped

Lemon pepper to taste

2 tablespoons parsley flakes

Mix mayonnaise and Chef Johnny's Herb Dressing in a large bowl. Add macaroni and mix. Add cucumbers, tomatoes, celery, and onion. Mix all ingredients well. Sprinkle in lemon pepper and mix. Refrigerate at least one hour.

Serve in chilled lettuce-lined bowl and sprinkle with parsley flakes.

BACON, LETTUCE, AND TOMATO SOUP

Serves 8

1 pound bacon, cut into 1-inch pieces
1 cup butter
6 large tomatoes, cut into wedges
2 tablespoons Pickapeppa Sauce
2 tablespoons Worcestershire sauce
2 tablespoons Tony's Seasoning
1 10-ounce can cream of asparagus soup
1 quart half-and-half
1 head of lettuce, cut into 1-inch pieces

Cook bacon in large saucepan. Remove bacon before crisp and set aside.

Add butter to bacon drippings and tomato wedges. Add Pickapeppa, Worcestershire sauce, and Tony's seasoning. Add soup and half-and-half and heat thoroughly, but do not allow to boil. Add bacon back to soup.

Serve over lettuce.

MANDY'S CHEESE-STUFFED MUSHROOMS

Serves 4 as appetizer

16 large mushrooms

2 tablespoons butter

2 tablespoons olive oil, combined with $\frac{1}{3}$ cup Italian breadcrumbs

4 tablespoons Johnny Jambalaya's Herb Dressing & Marinade

2 tablespoons Parmesan cheese, grated

1 cup onion, chopped

$\frac{1}{2}$ cup white wine

1 tablespoon garlic, minced

$\frac{1}{2}$ teaspoon parsley flakes

1 teaspoon lemon pepper

$\frac{1}{2}$ teaspoon Italian seasoning

2 tablespoons salsa

Pull stems out of mushroom caps. Set aside caps. Mince stems.

Place non-stick skillet over medium-low heat. When hot, add olive oil and 2 tablespoons of Herb Dressing & Marinade mixture and swirl in bottom of pan.

Once oil is hot, add onions and sauté 5 minutes until onions start to brown. Add garlic, chopped mushrooms stems, Italian seasoning, lemon pepper, parsley, and salsa. Stir and sauté 5 minutes.

Melt butter into mixture and stir in Italian breadcrumbs. Add cheese and stir. Remove from heat and allow to cool.

Preheat oven to 350 degrees. Spray large glass baking dish with Pam cooking spray. Stuff mushrooms with mixture and place in pan. Mix together wine and remaining 2 tablespoons Herb Dressing & Marinade and pour into bottom of pan. Cover with foil and bake for 30 minutes.

Uncover and bake 15 minutes more until browned.

Houmas House

Houmas House Plantation
and Gardens

40136 Highway 942

River Road

Darrow, Louisiana 70725

(225) 473-7841

www.houmashouse.com

The first owners of the plantation were the indigenous Houmas Indians, who were given a land grant to occupy the fertile plain between the Mississippi and Lake Maurepas to the north.

The Houmas sold the land to Maurice Conway and Alexander Latil in the mid-1700s. The original French provincial house that Latil erected on the property is situated directly behind the mansion, adjoined by a carriageway to the grand home described during its antebellum heyday as "The Sugar Palace." The original home was later used as living quarters for the mansion's staff.

By the time of the Louisiana Purchase in 1803, the plantation was established and producing sugar.

In 1810, Revolutionary War hero Gen. Wade Hampton of Virginia purchased the property and shortly thereafter began construction on the mansion. However, it was not until 1825 when Hampton's daughter, Caroline, and her husband, Col. John Preston, took over the property that the grand house truly began to take shape.

Construction on the mansion was completed in 1840. At the same time, Houmas House began to build its sugar production and continued to increase its land holdings, which ultimately grew to 300,000 acres.

Irishman John Burnside bought the plantation in 1857 for $1 million. A businessman and a character, Burnside increased production of sugar until Houmas House was the leading producer in the country, actively working the crop on 98,000 acres. During the Civil War, Burnside saved the mansion from destruction at the hands of advancing Union forces by declaring immunity as a subject of the British Crown. In addition to building a railway to carry his products to market—"The Sugar Cane Train (1862)"—Burnside, a bachelor, is also said to have offered payment to any parents in the parish who would name their sons "John."

An avid sportsman who wagered heavily in horse races, Burnside once secretly purchased a champion thoroughbred with the intent of defeating the steeds of fellow local businessmen in a big race. He quietly slipped the racehorse into the billiard room of the mansion where it was "stabled" until Burnside's surprise was unveiled at the starting line and hailed in the winner's circle.

Houmas House flourished under Burnside's ownership, but it was under his successor, Col. William Porcher Miles, that the plantation grew to its apex. In the late 1800s, it produced a monumental 20 million pounds of sugar each year.

In 1927, the Mississippi came out of its banks in the epic Great Flood. While Houmas House was spared, the surrounding areas were inundated. The ensuing economic havoc was but a prelude to the devastation of the Great Depression just two years later.

Houmas House Plantation withered away. The mansion closed and fell into disrepair until 1940 when Dr. George B. Crozat purchased it as a summer home. He renovated the property with the intent to give it a more "Federal" look than the stately Greek revival style. Crown moldings and ceiling medallions were removed and both interior and exterior forms and finishes were simplified.

Eventually, the Crozat heirs opened the property to tourists. In 1963, parts of the Bette Davis film *Hush, Hush Sweet Charlotte* were shot on the property. The room in which Ms. Davis stayed while filming is preserved as part of today's Houmas House tour.

In addition to the mansion and gardens, history is also reflected in the many antique furnishings and works of art that grace the Houmas House tour. Distinguished by its two Garconierre, the mansion exudes the warmth of a home (it is the owner's active residence) while proudly portraying its role as a landmark in American history.

Houmas House Plantation and Gardens has reclaimed its position as a jewel along Louisiana's River Road. Through the vision and determination of Kevin Kelly, who fulfilled a lifelong dream by acquiring the property in the spring of 2003, the mansion today reflects the best parts of each period in its rich history alongside the big bend in the Mississippi River.

CURRIED CHICKEN SALAD

Serves 6

1 ½ pounds boneless and skinless chicken,
cooked and cooled

1 cup plain yogurt

½ cup Dijon mustard

1 ½ tablespoons curry powder

½ tablespoon ground cumin

½ teaspoon cayenne pepper, plus more to taste

½ cup raisins

Kosher salt and freshly ground black pepper

½ cup pecans

Salad greens

Cut chicken into small cubes and set aside.
In a large bowl, combine yogurt, mustard, curry powder, cumin, and cayenne pepper. Add the cubed chicken and raisins. Season with salt, pepper, and more cayenne if desired. Mix in the pecans right before serving so they stay crunchy. Serve on a bed of greens as a salad.

FENNEL, ORANGE, SPINACH, AND OLIVE SALAD WITH SHAVED PARMESAN

Serves 4

1 large bulb fennel

3 navel oranges, peeled

¼ cup extra-virgin olive oil

2 tablespoons shallots, minced

½ teaspoon salt

¼ teaspoon freshly ground black pepper

2 cups baby spinach, stems removed, rinsed
well and patted dry

20 oil-cured black olives

2 ounces Parmesan, thinly shaved with a
vegetable peeler

Halve the fennel and thinly slice with a mandolin or very sharp knife. Segment the oranges over a bowl to catch any juices. Whisk together the orange juice, oil, shallots, salt, and pepper. Add the fennel, orange segments, and spinach, and toss to coat.

Divide the salad among 4 plates and top each with 5 olives. Top each salad with cheese.

SHRIMP AND ANDOUILLE-STUFFED QUAIL

Serves 4

2 tablespoons butter, plus more for coating quail

$^1/_2$ cup celery, chopped

1 cup onion, chopped

2 teaspoons thyme, chopped

1 teaspoon garlic, minced

$^1/_2$ pound shrimp, peeled and de-veined

$^1/_4$ pound andouille sausage, quartered and sliced

2 cups chicken or shrimp stock or broth

2 cups bread crumbs

$^1/_2$ cup green onion, chopped

3 tablespoons parsley leaves, chopped

Salt and pepper

8 semi-boneless quail (about 4 ounces each),
   split down the back

Preheat oven to 425 degrees. Melt butter in a sauté pan over medium heat and cook celery, onion, thyme, and garlic until wilted. Toss in shrimp and cook for 3 minutes. Add sausage to the pan, then stock.

Place breadcrumbs in a bowl and pour the shrimp mixture over. Stir to completely moisten, then add the green onions, parsley, and season with salt and pepper to taste.

Let stuffing cool and then divide into 8 portions. Wrap 1 quail around each portion, using toothpicks to secure the back. Rub each quail with a little butter and season with salt and pepper. Place quail on baking sheet and roast for 12–15 minutes until golden brown and firm, but not dry.

To serve, place 2 quails on each of 4 dinner plates.

Oak Alley

Oak Alley

3645 Hwy 18

Vacherie, Louisiana 70090

(225) 265-2151 or

(800) 44ALLEY

www.oakalleyplantation.com

In the beginning, there were the trees! Sometime in the early 1700s, probably a few years before the 1718 founding of New Orleans as the colonial seat of government, a settler claimed land from an original royal grant for his dwelling and lined its entrance with an alley of live oaks in two rows, leading to the river. Although we do not know how successful he was in his efforts to adapt in the New World, it is clear that his live oaks had no problem. Native to the area, they thrived; by 1722, when the early Capuchin Fathers arrived at St. Jacques de Cabahanoce to establish the settlement of St. James Parish, the young trees had already attained a stature which hinted at the magnificence that was to be theirs.

Into the bustle of development appeared Jacques Joseph Roman, the first known member of the Roman family in Louisiana. A native of Grenoble, France, he came to Louisiana to administer the affairs of his noble cousin Joseph Paris du Vernay, who had been granted a large concession of land up-river from New Orleans. In 1741, Jacques Joseph Roman married Marie D'Aigle, whose family had moved from Canada, and spent much of the first years of their marriage buying and selling plantations. Of their five children, only one son, Jacques Etienne, and his two sisters survived to inherit a sizeable estate.

Jacques Etienne married Marie Louise Patin, who enthusiastically presented him with a large family. The youngest, Jacques Telesphore, was born at the beginning of the nineteenth century into a colony whose fortune was flourishing, due in great part to successes in the field of sugar planting. Sugar quickly became the major crop along the Mississippi as far north as Baton Rouge.

Louisiana, meanwhile, had become a ping-pong ball on Spain and France's political table. In a few short weeks, Louisiana's flag changed from Spanish, who had claimed it since the transfer from French hands by secret treaty in 1763, to the French tri-color, to the Stars and Stripes. It remained in America's hands, finally achieving statehood in 1812. However, in the three brief weeks of the post-revolution French regime (November 30–December 20, 1803), the Napoleonic Code was introduced,

establishing a precedent that would create a distinct legal system in Louisiana.

The word Creole is a derivative of the Spanish *criollo,* meaning "native-born," and was used to denote children of European parentage born in the New World. French Creoles such as the Romans viewed their new countrymen with disdain, claiming they had no refinement at all, and withdrew into New Orleans' Vieux Carré (or Old Square), where the French language and old ways prevailed. However, as more and more Americans poured into the area, a compromise became inevitable and the cultures began to merge.

As the Roman children grew up and married, the family achieved more prominence as leaders of society, and their activities alternated between their plantations in St. James Parish and elegant dwellings in New Orleans. Among the latter was the house now known as Madame John's Legacy on Rue Dumaine. From here, Jacques Telesphore Roman began his courtship of Celina Pilie, whose prominent family lived around the corner on Rue Royal. They were married in June of 1834. On May 19, 1836, ownership of Oak Alley Plantation was transferred to J.T. Roman, in exchange for the nearby Roman family estate and cancellation of a bank debt.

Much later, Hollywood discovered Oak Alley with productions such as *Hush, Hush, Sweet Charlotte* (with Bette Davis), *Interview with a Vampire,* starring Tom Cruise and Brad Pitt, and *Primary Colors,* starring John Travolta.

153

PESTO CHEESECAKE

Serves 8

$^1/_2$ tablespoon butter at room temperature

$^1/_4$ cup fine Italian breadcrumbs

$^1/_4$ cup plus 1 tablespoon freshly grated
Parmesan cheese

1 8-ounce package cream cheese

$^1/_2$ cup ricotta cheese

$^1/_8$ teaspoon salt

$^1/_8$ teaspoon cayenne pepper

2 large eggs

$^1/_4$ cup purchased pesto sauce

$^1/_8$ cup pine nuts

Preheat oven to 325 degrees. Rub 1 tablespoon butter over bottom and sides of 9-inch pan.

Mix breadcrumbs with 2 tablespoons grated Parmesan cheese. Coat pan with mixture.

Using electric mixer, beat cream cheese, ricotta, remaining Parmesan, salt, and cayenne pepper in large bowl until light. Add eggs, one at a time, beating well after each addition.

Transfer half of mixture to medium bowl, mix pesto into remaining half and pour into prepared 9-inch pan. Smooth top carefully. Spoon plain mixture over top, smooth and sprinkle with pine nuts.

Bake until center no longer moves when shaken (about 45 minutes). Transfer from oven and cool completely. Cover tightly with plastic and refrigerate overnight.

Run knife around edge to loosen. Garnish with basil.

BANANAS FOSTER FRENCH TOAST

Serves 4

Bananas Foster Syrup

1 ½ cups good-quality maple syrup

2 tablespoons butter

4 bananas, peeled, halved, and sliced
  lengthwise

1 teaspoon rum flavoring (extract) or 1
  tablespoon dark rum

In a small saucepan, heat syrup over medium heat. Add butter and stir until melted and syrup is bubbling. Add bananas and heat thoroughly.

Remove from heat and add rum or rum extract. Return to slow heat and keep warm.

French Toast

6 large eggs

2 teaspoons vanilla

½ cup heavy cream

6 tablespoons butter

8 slices French bread (preferably a few days old)

To make batter, whisk eggs, then add vanilla. Pour in cream and whisk until well blended.

Melt 1–2 tablespoons of butter over medium-high heat.

Dip slices of bread into batter and soak thoroughly. Place 2 slices at a time in melted butter and cook each side until golden brown. Repeat with remaining slices.

Serve slices with warm syrup and bananas.

155

Myrtles Plantation

The 209-year-old Myrtles Plantation was built by General David "Whiskey Dave" Bradford around 1796. General Bradford was labeled "Whiskey Dave" for his participation in the Whiskey Rebellion. He deserted George Washington's Army to avoid being arrested and imprisoned or, worse, shot as a traitor.

Bradford surfaced at Bayou Sara, then a Spanish colony, and obtained a land grant for 650 acres. Feeling safe in this remote territory, Whiskey Dave started a new life and a family. Construction of the plantation got off to a prophetic start when he accidentally plowed into a Tunica Indian burial ground, laying the planks for the plantation's big house. Eventually, his daughter Sara Matilda grew up and married Judge Clark Woodruff. They moved into the Myrtles in 1834.

As was common for slave owners of the day, Judge Woodruff used the female house slave, Chloe, for a bed warmer. Wife Sara ignored the situation, possibly encouraging Chloe to become possessive. She was caught eavesdropping on her master by listening through a door and, as punishment, he cut off her left ear.

In retaliation, Chloe baked a birthday cake laced with oleander for the Judge's wife and two daughters. The leaves of the oleander plant are poisonous; all three died a horrible death of cramps and fits. She pleaded that she only intended to make them sick so she could nurse them back to health, but this did not sway the vigilantes. They hung her from one of the large oak trees near the main house. Her ghost is said to haunt the plantation.

The Myrtles has been written about in *The New York Times*, *Forbes*, *Gourmet*, *Veranda*, *Travel and Leisure*, *Country Inns*, *Colonial Homes*, and *Delta SKY*. It has also been featured on *Oprah*, *A & E*, *The History Channel*, *The Travel Channel*, *The Learning Channel*, *National Geographic Explorer*, and *Good Morning, America*.

Throughout its history, the house passed through many families and was eventually restored in the 1970s. Its current owners run an 11-room bed and breakfast on the property. Historical tours are conducted daily from 9am–5pm.

Myrtles Plantation

US Hwy 61 N

St. Francisville, Louisiana 70775

(800) 809-0565 or

(225) 635-6277

www.myrtlesplantation.com

156

Mystery tours are conducted on Friday and Saturday evenings.

All bed and breakfast reservations include a complimentary tour of this National Historic Register home, which is filled with hand painted stained glass, open pierced plaster frieze work, Aubusson tapestries, Baccarat crystal chandeliers, Carrera marble mantles, and gold-leafed French furnishings.

The history of the South will always provide tales of romance and mystery, and Myrtles Plantation offers its guests a chance to relive these moments by stepping back in time into the days of the Antebellum South. A first glimpse of the mansion, with its magnificent double dormers and moss draped oaks, envelopes one in peace and tranquility.

Relax in the giant rockers on the 120-foot verandah or stroll through the lush gardens. The 5000-square-foot brick courtyard is the perfect place to unwind before enjoying a delicious candlelight dinner at the Carriage House Restaurant.

CHICKEN AND DUMPLINGS

Serves 4

3 pounds boneless, skinless chicken breast meat, cut into 2-inch chunks
3 cans cream of mushroom soup
4 cups chicken broth
16-ounce can Pet milk
3 cups 2-percent milk
¼ cup butter
8 boiled eggs, sliced
Tony Chachere Seasoning to taste
Freshly ground black pepper to taste
1 mixture of your favorite biscuit dough

Roll out biscuit dough and cut into 1-inch by 4-inch strips. Flour both sides of each strip so that they don't stick together.

Mix soup, broth, milk, and butter in a big heavy-bottomed pot. Add chicken and simmer for 20 minutes.

Add dough strips, egg slices, and Tony Chachere Seasoning. Add more milk if needed. It will thicken as it cooks.

Enjoy!

GAMMY'S 9-MINUTE MICROWAVE PECAN BRITTLE

Yields 1 pound

1 cup sugar
½ cup light corn syrup
⅛ teaspoon salt
1½ cups pecans (may be roasted)
1 tablespoon butter
1 teaspoon vanilla
1 teaspoon baking soda

Combine sugar, syrup, and salt in 2-quart glass container. Microwave on high for 5 minutes.

Stir in pecans and microwave for 4 minutes. Syrup will turn light brown.

Stir in butter, vanilla, and soda until light and foamy. Spread to ¼-inch thickness on well-buttered or Pam-sprayed cookie sheet.

Cool. Break into bite size pieces.

MUSCADINE JAM

3 ¹/₂ cups muscadine pulp

5 ¹/₄ cups sugar

¹/₄ cup sweet wine (any kind)

1 envelope Sure-jell powder

Wash muscadines, cut in half, and mash. Do not peel.

Simmer for 15–20 minutes. They may have enough fluid if they are juicy; if not, add a little water.

Pass through a food mill to remove seeds and skin.

Measure out remaining muscadine pulp to be sure you have 3½ cups.

To Sure-jell powder, add ¾ cups water and boil for one minute. Add in muscadine pulp mixture and stir for 3 minutes.

Store refrigerated in clean, sterile jars. Will keep for a few weeks.

Muscadine is a North American grape with a strong flavor and a thick skin. Easy to grow, it makes wonderful jams and wines. It is usually sold at all country fairs and fruit markets.

159

The Cabin

The Cabin

Corner of Hwy 44 & Hwy 22

Burnside, Louisiana 70737

(225) 473-3007

The Cabin restaurant is unique in that it began as one of the ten original slave dwellings of the Monroe Plantation. It is approximately 150 years old. Upon entering the Cabin, one notices an aura of authenticity and realism. The original cypress roof is still visible from inside, and the spider webs of 100 years ago still cling to the ceiling. The roof is supported by four massive beams—manufacturer's rejects, obtained in trade for a bottle of Old Crow bourbon. Ancient newspapers are stuck to the wall with a mixture of flour and water. This was the way the slaves insulated the walls of the original slave dwelling. Antique farm implements and tools of years gone by hang from every nook and cranny. The original floor in the main cabin has been replaced with pine flooring from the commissary at the Welham Plantation in Convent.

"Rock" the alligator was carved from a virgin cypress sinker log. This log was cut down approximately 100–120 years ago on the banks of the Amite River. It had been lying on the riverbed under mud since then. It was retrieved on April 20, 1988, and sculpted by James Schexnaydre into the "Largest Alligator in the World."

The extension to the rear of the main cabin is a two-room slave dwelling from the Welham Plantation, its original roof and walls intact. It is approximately 140 years old. To the rear of this cabin are the restrooms, which are unique in their own way: they were constructed from a cypress water cistern that was used to store fresh rainwater. The partitions in the restrooms are from the Old Crow Distillery in New Orleans, which was demolished in 1970.

The main dining room—built onto the back of the Cabin to resemble a garconnier (the visiting bachelor's quarters on a river road plantation)—opens via French doors to a brick courtyard surrounded by two more slave cabins, both from the Helvelta Plantation. The area is dominated by the restored Schoolhouse, the first black Catholic school in Louisiana, built in 1865 by the sisters of the Sacred Heart, This treasure is registered as a national historic property.

The Cabin serves meals typical of the River Road tradition, while at the same time preserving some of the local farm history.

TURTLE SOUP

Serves 10–12

2 pounds turtle meat

3 tablespoons cooking oil

2 large onions, chopped

$^1/_2$ cup bell pepper, chopped

1 cup celery, chopped

2 cloves garlic, minced

4 bay leaves

1 cup tomato paste

2 tablespoons flour

1 cup water

2 quarts water

2 tablespoons salt

1 tablespoon cayenne pepper

1 tablespoon Worcestershire sauce

$^1/_2$ cup parsley, minced

Lemon slices

1 egg, hard-boiled

Season turtle meat and fry in oil until brown on all sides. Add a little bit of water to prevent from sticking. Add onions, bell peppers, garlic, and bay leaves. Stir frequently and continue frying. Cook till onions are tender.

As this continues to cook, add the tomato paste and stir. Sprinkle the flour over the entire pot and stir. Continue stirring and add in one cup of water. Cook for 30 minutes. Stir occasionally.

Add 2 quarts of water, salt, and cayenne pepper, and bring to a boil. Let simmer at boiling point for 1 hour. When meat is fully tender, add the Worcestershire and parsley. Garnish with lemon slices and hard-boiled egg. Sprinkle with parsley and serve.

Butter Beans with Shrimp

Serves 20–24

1 gallon water

2 cups brown roux, prepared

2 medium yellow onions, finely chopped

1 cup green onions, chopped

1 large green bell pepper, chopped

3 ribs celery, chopped

1 can Rotel Tomatoes Diced w/ Green Chilies

4 pounds frozen baby lima beans

Seasonall to taste

5 pounds shrimp, peeled

Granulated garlic

Black pepper

Cooked rice

In a large, heavy-bottomed stockpot, bring water to a boil. Dissolve roux in water. Lower fire to a simmer and add chopped vegetables and Rotel tomatoes. Add frozen baby lima beans and add seasoning to taste. Allow to simmer about 45 minutes to an hour.

Add shrimp and cover the pot. Cook until shrimp turn pink. Serve over hot rice.

Yam and Pecan Pie

Yields 4 pies

1 cup butter

2 cups brown sugar

$1/2$ teaspoon salt

12 eggs

3 cups corn syrup

4 cups yams, cooked and mashed

6 cups pecans

4 pie shells

1 teaspoon cinnamon

$1/2$ teaspoon nutmeg

1 teaspoon vanilla

Cream butter and sugar together. Add salt, eggs, corn syrup, yams, and vanilla. Beat until well blended.

Spread one cup of pecans in bottom of each pie shell. Pour mixture over pecans, and then sprinkle ½ cup pecans over top of each pie.

Bake at 375 degrees for 50–55 minutes.

*"The only real stumbling block is fear of failure.
In cooking you've got to have a what-the-hell attitude."*
Julia Child

Ponchatoulas

Ponchatoulas

109 E Park Ave

Ruston, Louisiana 71270

(318) 254-5200

Ruston, Louisiana, parish seat of Lincoln Parish, is located in the north-central part of the state, about 35 miles south of Arkansas. Ask anyone what the population is and you will get a blank look and an estimated "around 20,000" as an answer. The confusion arises from the practice of counting the students enrolled in Louisiana Tech University as part of the population. The university's enrollment normally stands at approximately 6,500.

Ruston sprang to life in 1884 when the Vicksburg, Shreveport, and Pacific Railroad completed laying its tracks across North Louisiana. Merchants from nearby communities built tents and temporary shelters and supplied food, clothing, and hardware to the construction crew. It seemed there was profit to be gained by settling near the railroad, and they persuaded property owner Robert E. Russ to supply a town site.

Surveyors for the railroad laid out the streets. Numbers drawn from a hat assigned the town lots, which were sold for $375 each. The business district emerged, and Russ Town was founded.

Cotton was the basic industry. Farmers took their crop to Ruston to be ginned and compressed, and the railroad transported the bales of cotton to market. The town slowly grew.

Ponchatoulas has the distinction of being housed in the first fire station in Ruston. The interior still resembles the inside of a fire house. Sit at the bar and imagine where the trucks were parked in days gone by, or try and figure out where the fireman's pole was located.

The building itself is over 70 years old, and it has served various purposes. For a period of time, the ground floor was the site of a Sears store. At another time, it was a funeral home. The third floor was the location of the radio station KRUS, which helped inform and entertain residents for many years. Currently, that same top floor houses a recording studio.

For ten years, locals have flocked to Ponchatoulas for a good meal and a good time. The owners chose this name because of a visit to the town of the same name—Ponchatoula, Louisiana—which they liked very much.

WHITE BEANS

Serves 6–8

1 pound dried navy beans

2 whole bay leaves

1 teaspoon Tabasco

$^1/_4$ teaspoon cayenne

2 teaspoons garlic, minced

$^1/_2$ pound ham, chopped

2 cups onions, finely chopped

$^3/_4$ tablespoon sugar

1 tablespoon liquid smoke

1 $^1/_2$ teaspoons salt

Combine all ingredients except salt in pot. Add enough water to boil the beans. Boil until beans are soft (easily mashed with a fork).

When beans are soft, add salt and serve.

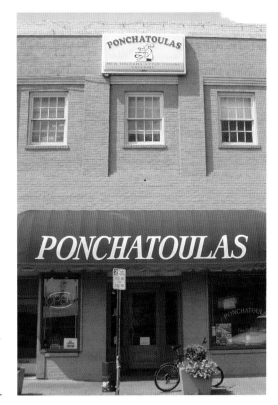

BOUDIN

Yields 10–12 pounds

6 pounds boneless pork

1 pound pork liver

12 cups cooked rice

2 teaspoons salt

$^1/_2$ teaspoon black pepper

$^1/_2$ teaspoon cayenne

6 cups onions

2 cups green onions, chopped

Casing for sausage

Cook pork and pork liver until tender. Reserve gravy.

Grind meat and liver with chili blade.

Mix all ingredients and gravy.

Stuff casing.

After casing is stuffed, boil Boudin in water on low heat for 5 minutes to set casing.

Mabry House

Built in 1902 by William Alexander Mabry, Mabry House is listed on the National Register of Historic Places. The interior of the house features a magnificent stairway with a fine carved balustrade and large, airy rooms with high ceilings.

A city councilman in the late 1890s, W.A. Mabry was a successful grocer and a partner in the firm of Goldstein Mabry & Co. He later decided to study law and was a practicing attorney in Shreveport. From 1912–1916 he was Caddo Parish District Attorney and later served as an interim Caddo District Court Judge. The house had been divided into apartments in the 1930s after Mr. Mabry's wife died. It remained in the family until 1968, when it was sold to Dr. Ollie Williams.

Mabry House exchanged hands several times before Steve and Ginger Mylar purchased it in January 2002, in anticipation of opening a fine dining restaurant. In April 2002, after some remodeling and the addition of a full kitchen, Mabry House was open for business. Chef and owner Steve Mylar boasts over 20 years of kitchen experience. After graduating from culinary school in Philadelphia, he worked in fine restaurants and private clubs in Pennsylvania, Florida, Texas, and Louisiana before purchasing Mabry House. The restaurant offers great continental cuisine with a varying menu that includes Cajun fare as well as cuisine of oriental and island influence.

Mabry House

1540 Irving Place

Shreveport, Louisiana 71101

(318) 227-1121

SPICED BUTTERNUT SQUASH SOUP

Serves 20–24

1 large butternut squash (about 3 pounds)

1 large yellow onion

1 clove garlic, minced

4 tablespoons oil

Chicken broth to cover (about 2 quarts)

2 cinnamon sticks

2 star anise

4 whole cloves

1 quart heavy cream

Salt and white pepper to taste

Peel and seed squash and cut into large dice.

Sauté onion and garlic in oil until transparent. Add squash and chicken broth to cover.

Tie cinnamon sticks, star anise, and cloves in a cheesecloth bundle. Add bundle to squash mixture and bring to a boil. Simmer until very soft.

Remove spice bundle and purée mixture until smooth.

Return to heat and add cream. Season with salt and pepper to taste.

CHILI AND CUMIN-RUBBED SALMON

Serves 4

4 salmon fillets (about 7 ounces each),
   skin removed

2 tablespoons oil

1 medium red onion, chopped

1 clove garlic, minced

2 cups tomato concasse

3 tablespoons dark brown sugar

2 tablespoons fresh lime juice

2 tablespoons white vinegar

1 tablespoon honey

2 tablespoons dark chili powder

1 tablespoon ground cumin

$1/2$ teaspoon each white, red, and black pepper

Salt to taste

2 tablespoons chopped fresh cilantro

Sauté onion in oil until transparent. Add tomato concasse and cook until soft, about 10 minutes.

Add remaining ingredients except cilantro. Simmer for about 20 minutes until thick. Let cool.

Pour mixture into food processor and purée. Stir in cilantro.

Brush heavily on salmon fillet and let marinate for 30 minutes.

Brush grill with oil and grill 3–4 minutes per side, basting as needed.

167

Strawn's Eat Shop

Strawn's Eat Shop

125 Kings Hwy

Shreveport, Louisiana 71104

(318) 868-0634

Captain Henry Miller Shreve, who was responsible for clearing the Red River of a logjam, founded Shreveport in 1839. The area quickly flourished and Bossier City was founded in the 1840s as a small trading post. It was first known as Cane's Landing and was briefly referred to both as Alexander's Precinct and Caneville.

Shreveport and Bossier City are sister cities connected by the Red River. The combined population of the two cities is almost 350,000. Modern times have made Shreveport-Bossier City, with its five casinos and horserace track, a popular gaming destination.

The Red River District is a hub of entertainment, restaurants, clubs, and shops on Shreveport's riverfront. Across the river, Bossier City offers its entertainment venue, Louisiana Boardwalk.

Shreveport-Bossier City relies on Claude the Cajun Crawfish to predict the party weather for Mardi Gras. Each year, everyone gathers around the dirt-mound home of Claude, a live crawfish. When Claude is ready, he'll climb to the top of his burrow. If he waves his claws to the sky, everyone can expect party weather. If

he doesn't, he's thrown into a steaming pot of hot gumbo nearby. Some suggest that Groundhog Day should be renamed, because Claude has never gotten it wrong (this may be because, at Mardi Gras time, people will party in any kind of weather).

Shreveport hosts Barksdale Air Force Base, home of the mighty B-52s. This was the military installation from which President George W. Bush first addressed the nation following the September 11 attacks.

Shreveport spawned a superstar on October 16, 1954. Elvis Presley got his start on the Louisiana Hayride, a radio program that was broadcasted from the Municipal Auditorium.

A classic diner choice for breakfast or lunch in Shreveport is Strawn's Eat Shop, known for its delicious icebox pies, home-style fried chicken dinners, and crispy hash browns, not to mention a great view of Centenary College. The pie is so good, locals are in and out of the restaurant all day long, buying whole pies and slices to go. In 1944, Mr. Strawn opened his doors on King's Highway. He was an immediate success. In the mid-'50s, he sold Strawn's to his good friend Gus Alexander. At the time, the small diner only sat 57 people. In 1988, Buddy Gauthier bought the diner from Gus, who was ready to retire. (It was not won in a poker game as some local legends say.)

Buddy and Nancy Gauthier have owned and operated the store since then, doubling the seating capacity. Success has lead to a feature article in *Southern Living* about the restaurant's world-famous pies. In 2003, their fried chicken was also featured on *Food Network's* "Best of Blue Plate Specials."

Daughter Celeste Gauthier opened a second location of Strawn's called Strawn's Eat Shop TOO! in 2002. In 2004, daughter Heather opened a third location, Strawn's Eat Shop, in Bossier City.

What makes Strawn's successful is a true love of family and heart. Several of their employees worked for over 30 years until they retired. Catherine Jackson, current head cook for all three locations, trained under the Strawn's original cook for several years.

Heather Gautier says, "I personally have employees working for me who have known me since I was seven years of age. The caring they have shown me and my family is truly amazing. I always tell my customers who question my owning a business at the young age of 23 that I might be young, but I have over 15 years of experiences."

"I look upon it that he who does not mind his belly, will hardly mind anything else."
Samuel Johnson

SCALLOPED POTATOES

Serves 10–12

3 pounds red potatoes, peeled and sliced

$1/2$ cup butter

2 teaspoons salt

1 teaspoon black pepper

2 teaspoons granulated garlic

$1/2$ cup flour

$1/2$ cup onions, diced

Preheat oven to 350 degrees.

Spread half of potatoes in a layer at the bottom of a deep pan. Add half of each of the butter, salt, pepper, garlic, and flour.

Add second half of potatoes and repeat the adding of ingredients. Add the onions to the top of the pan.

Cover pan with foil and cook in oven for 1 hour.

STRAWN'S PIE CRUST

Yields double crusts for 2 pies

4 cups all-purpose flour

1 teaspoon salt

$1/2$ cup sugar

$1 1/2$ cups shortening

12 ounces chilled water

Preheat oven to 300 degrees.

In a large bowl, mix flour, salt, sugar, and shortening. Mix in chilled water in small amounts until dough is blended.

Roll into 9-inch pie pans.

Bake at 300 degrees for 45 minutes until golden brown.

> *"Part of the secret of success in life is to eat what you like, and let the food fight it out inside."*
> Mark Twain

CHICKEN AND DUMPLINGS

Chicken

1 hen

2 teaspoons salt

1 teaspoon black pepper

½ cup onions, chopped

2 teaspoons chicken base

Water to cover

Boil the chicken in the broth until done.

Remove chicken from broth, debone, and cut into large pieces. (Do not discard broth.)

Dumplings

4 cups all-purpose flour, divided

1 teaspoon salt

4 eggs

12 ounces boiling water

½ cup butter

Mix 2 cups flour with remaining ingredients until a sticky dough forms. Add reserved 2 cups of flour to mixture.

Roll dough out and cut into squares. Drop squares into the reserved boiling chicken broth and cook until dough is tender.

Mix in the chicken and serve.

171

The Landing

The Landing

530 Front Street

Natchitoches, Louisiana 71457

(318) 352-1579

The people and businesses in Natchitoches have built an impressive industry around their standing as the oldest city in Louisiana and the oldest permanent settlement in the Louisiana Purchase territory. The city of Natchitoches is located in the parish of the same name. One of nine incorporated areas within the parish, Natchitoches is by far the most famous. It was founded in 1714, two years before New Orleans, by French Canadian Louis Antoine Juchereau de St. Denis.

Other incorporated areas of the parish include Ashland, Campti, Clarence, Goldonna, Natchez, Powhatan, Provencal, and Robeline. Ashland was not incorporated until 1963, even though the area was settled around 1899.

Provencal was incorporated in 1890 and was named after a settler, Alfred Provencal. Campti was named after a Natchitoches Indian chief, and Natchez was named after an Indian tribe. But while Campti was friendly toward the settlers, the Natchez tribe was not. The tribe was driven out of the area and defeated.

In addition to its history, Natchitoches also is famous for its annual Christmas Festival of Lights. The Christmas tradition started in 1926, when electrician Max Burgdof persuaded local city officials and business officials to string up some Christmas lights.

Natchitoches has repeatedly been named one of the top places to retire in the United States by *Kiplinger's* magazine and *Where to Retire* magazine. It was also listed in the book *100 Best Small Art Towns in America* and was named one of 12 great road trips in the United States by *National Geographic Traveler*. Oprah Winfrey did a show from Natchitoches, calling it "the best little town in the USA." It also gained fame as the site for the filming of "Steel Magnolias" in 1988.

Today, Natchitoches is a major tourist destination. The historic district consists of 33 blocks on the National Historic Register. It includes more than 50 buildings built more than a century ago. The district also includes Fort St. Jean Baptiste, the fort built two years after St. Denis arrived. Another big draw is Cane River Lake, a body of water that was part of the Red River and was a steamboat route until the river changed course in the early 1800s.

The historic downtown area has also been named a National Landmark District. There are only two National Landmark Districts in the state. (The other is the Vieux Carré in New Orleans, more commonly know as the French Quarter.) The Landing is located in one of the original buildings constructed along Front Street.

VOODOO OYSTERS

Very hot appetizer.

Serves 2

Cornmeal mixture

1 cup cornmeal
1 cup cornflour
1 teaspoon garlic powder
1 teaspoon cayenne pepper
1 teaspoon seasoned salt
1 teaspoon black pepper

Mix all ingredients together.

Butter mixture

4 ounces clear butter
1 tablespoon black pepper
1 tablespoon granulated garlic
$1/2$ tablespoon onion powder
$1 1/2$ tablespoons salt
$1/2$ tablespoon oregano leaf
$1/2$ tablespoon thyme
1 tablespoon paprika

Melt butter and mix well with other ingredients. Reserve warm on stove.

Oysters

1 dozen oysters
2 cups all-purpose flour
4 cups water

Dredge oysters in flour, drop in water, and dredge again in cornmeal mixture.

Deep-fry oysters at 350 degrees for about 45 seconds, until golden brown.

Heat butter mixture until simmering.

To serve, place oysters on a bed of hot white rice and pour butter mixture over the oysters. Sprinkle with fresh lemon juice.

CRAB-CLAW MARINADE

Yields marinade for 2 pounds

$1/3$ cup green onion, minced
$1/4$ cup fresh parsley, chopped
2 ribs celery, chopped
1 clove garlic, minced
$1/3$ cup olive oil
2 tablespoons lemon juice
$1/4$ cup tarragon vinegar
$1/2$ cup green olives, chopped

Place all ingredients in a food processor and chop fine. Let stand for 24 hours before using.

CANE RIVER FREEZE

Serves 1

2 scoops vanilla ice cream
1 ounce dark Cream de Cacao
1 teaspoon coffee grounds

Place ice cream in serving glass. Pour Cream de Cacao over ice cream. Sprinkle coffee over ice cream.

Bailey Hotel

Bailey Hotel

200 W. Magnolia St.

Bunkie, Louisiana 71322

(318) 346 7111

(866) 346 7111

Deep in the heart of Louisiana sits the historic Bailey Hotel, where turn-of-the-century style and Cajun hospitality come together. Located in Bunkie, The Bailey Hotel, built in 1907, is located at the Crossroads of Louisiana.

Central Louisiana—Avoyelles Parish in particular—advertises itself as one of the most easy-going places in the world. The local people are hard-working and friendly, and their unique outlook on life makes all guests feel welcome. Bunkie is primarily a farming community, so you will find many early risers in the dining room of The Bailey at 5 a.m., wide-awake and enjoying a home-cooked breakfast.

Central Louisiana is also a hunter's paradise. It is often referred to as Duck Hunting Haven. Toledo Bend Reservoir is the mother of many skiing and fishing recreational parks.

The town of Bunkie received its name in a rather unusual fashion. In 1882, the Texas and Pacific Railroad was laid through the area and a small station was established. Mr. Haas was given the privilege of naming this station and the town. He chose "Bunkie," the nickname of his little girl, who mispronounced the word "monkey" to describe a toy brought to her from New Orleans by her father.

Gourmet chefs prepare local cuisine in true southern style at the Bailey, where Cajun cooking is alive and well. With homemade biscuits, honey-cured ham and bacon, omelets to order, grits, and pancakes, along with fresh fruits and juice, one need not look any further for an old-fashioned breakfast. Dinner is prepared by experienced chefs and sauciers who exemplify the elegance of southern dining.

Entertainment occurs nightly in Zanga's, the hotel lounge. Named for Professor Zanga, a soothsayer and clairvoyant who stayed in room 39 in 1925, the lounge allows guests to step back in time and experience true New Orleans with jazz, contemporary and true Avoyelles Parish music being performed weekly.

The Bailey Hotel has been the center of community activity. Domino tournaments and bridge games have drawn their share of willing contestants. The past can be revisited, old friendships can be reunited, and new acquaintances can be sparked with the flint of the past.

Tomato and Goat Cheese Salad
with Basil/Kalamata Olive Vinaigrette

Serves 4

2 8-ounce bags mixed gourmet salad greens

8 ripe tomatoes (Roma are best)

16 ounces goat cheese (preferably fresh)

1 red onion, sliced

Basil/Kalamata olive vinaigrette (recipe follows)

Place lettuce mix on chilled salad plates. Layer sliced tomato, goat cheese, and red onion slices. Repeat layers as desired. Top with vinaigrette.

Basil/Kalamata Olive Vinaigrette

4 ounces fresh basil

4 or 5 cloves fresh garlic

$^3/_4$ cup pitted Kalamata olives.

1 cup extra-virgin olive oil

$^1/_2$ cup red wine vinegar

1 teaspoon salt

$^1/_2$ teaspoon black pepper

Combine all ingredients in a food processor or blender until smooth.

Roast Duck and Andouille Pasta

Serves 4

Meat from 1 roast duck

1 pound mushrooms, sliced

$^1/_2$ cup green onions, chopped

$^1/_4$ cup butter

$^1/_2$ teaspoon Cavender's Greek Seasoning

$^1/_2$ teaspoon granulated garlic

$^1/_4$ cup dry red wine

2 cups heavy cream

$^1/_2$ cup shredded parmesan cheese

16 ounces pasta (preferably bow tie), cooked al dente

1 pound Andouille sausage

Melt butter in skillet. Add mushrooms and Andouille sausage. Sauté until mushrooms and sausage are done. Add green onions and continue cooking until onions wilt.

Add duck, Cavender's Greek Seasoning, and garlic.

Deglaze pan with wine. Add heavy cream and reduce until mixture coats a spoon.

Place warm pasta in large bowl or casserole. Add sauce and toss to coat pasta. Serve immediately, with parmesan cheese to taste.

177

Lasyone's Meat Pie Restaurant

Lasyone's Meat Pie Restaurant is a favorite of locals and travelers alike. This family-owned and operated restaurant is famous for its meat pies. You'll feel like a real Louisiana native the moment you walk through the door and take in the aroma of good, down-home cooking.

Though the meat pie is as old as the Civil War, it only recently gained fame in the hands of James Lasyone. More than 3 decades ago, Mr. Lasyone rented out the bottom half of a building that once was the home to the Phoenix Lodge #38, built in 1859. While the masons still occupied the top portion of the building, James Lasyone started his Meat Pie Kitchen. He convinced some of the town's ladies to sell him a few of their meat pies. He did a little experimenting and came up with one of his own. People from all over the world have stopped in to try Lasyone's meat pie, including Lorne Greene, Vanna White, Daryl Hannah, and a host of others.

Lasyone's Meat Pie has been recognized and raved about by a score of magazines, including *Southern Living, The New Yorker, Glamour,* and *Gourmet.* Representatives from major newspapers such as *The Houston Chronicle, Times-Picayune New Orleans, The Dallas Morning News, Chicago Tribune,* and international papers from France, Italy, and Spain have found their way to Lasyone's Meat Pie Restaurant. It has also been featured in segments of *On the Road with Charles Kuralt* and *Good Morning, America* with Bryant Gumble.

Although the meat pie is Lasyone's most popular offering, it is not the only treat on the menu. The Cane River Cream Pie is another delight for the taste buds. It was discovered completely by accident when chocolate milk was used instead of white milk. The restaurant's dirty rice, red beans and sausage, chicken and dumplings, and other well-known Louisiana Cajun and Creole cuisine are Lasyone family specialties.

Family chefs James and his daughter Angela run the kitchen, and all the food is made the old fashioned way. With its down-home atmosphere and old family recipes, Lasyone's Restaurant makes you feel like part of the family.

Lasyone's Meat Pie Restaurant

622 Second Street

Natchitoches, Louisiana

(318) 352-3353

www.lasyones.com

178

CHICKEN AND DUMPLINGS

Serves 6

1 cut-up chicken

Water

1 teaspoon Accent

1 1/2 teaspoons salt

1/4 teaspoon black pepper

1/2 teaspoon powdered garlic

1 medium onion, chopped

2 ribs celery, chopped

1 cup sweet milk

Dough

2 cups self-rising flour

1 1/2 cups sweet milk

1 tablespoon parsley flakes

1 or 2 drops yellow food coloring (optional)

Put chicken in large heavy pot and cover with water (You must have plenty of stock). Add seasoning salt, salt, black pepper, garlic, onion, and celery to pot and boil until chicken is tender.

Remove chicken from pot and de-bone. Then return stock to medium heat, adding 1 cup of milk.

To make the dough: Add parsley flakes to flour; mix. Add enough milk to make a stiff dough. If you want a more yellow-colored dumpling, add one or two drops of yellow food coloring to the milk used in the dough.

Make a ball using a lightly floured board. Roll dough to about 1/8-inch thickness and cut into 1 1/2-inch strips.

As stock begins to boil, drop in about half of dumplings and let cook about 10 minutes before dropping the last half. Be sure broth is boiling before you start dropping the dumplings. Add hot water if you need more broth. Reduce heat and simmer for about 15 minutes.

Add de-boned chicken to dumplings before serving.

179

LASYONE'S RED BEANS AND SAUSAGE

Serves 8–10

1 pound dry red kidney beans (picked and washed)

$^1/_2$ cup Wesson oil or bacon drippings

$^1/_2$ cup dry parsley flakes

10 cups water

1 teaspoon Accent seasoning salt

2 teaspoons salt

1 medium bell pepper, chopped

2 ribs of celery, chopped

2 tablespoons sugar

$^1/_4$ teaspoon red pepper

1 teaspoon granulated garlic

1 cup smoked sausage, chopped

In a 4-quart pot, combine all of the above ingredients except the smoked sausage. Add smoked sausage in the last 30 minutes of cooking time.

Cook uncovered over medium heat for approximately 2 hours or until beans are tender. More water may be added as needed.

Serve over fluffy white rice.

For additional sausage, cut smoked sausage in links and pan fry. Place on top of red beans and rice to serve.

LASYONE'S DIRTY RICE

Serves approximately 15

$^1/_2$ cup vegetable oil

$^1/_2$ pound ground beef

1 pound ground chicken gizzards

1 tablespoon parsley flakes

1 teaspoon Accent (optional)

2 tablespoon Kitchen Bouquet (for darkening)

$^1/_4$ cup chicken broth

1 small jar chopped pimento

Salt and pepper to taste

1 large onion, medium chopped

1 large bell pepper, medium chopped

3 ripe celery, medium chopped

1 cup green onion tops, medium chopped

6 cloves garlic, medium chopped

6 cups cooked rice

Heat oil in Dutch oven. Add beef and gizzards. Cook until gray in color. Add all other ingredients except rice. Simmer for 20 minutes.

Pour mixture over rice and fold just enough to mix well. Cover with foil. Bake for 40 minutes at 325 degrees or until rice has absorbed all liquid.

Note: You can cook the mixture the day before. The next day just add rice and bake.

CRAWFISH ÉTOUFFÉE

Serves 6–8

2 heaping tablespoons plain flour

Enough Wesson oil to make roux
  (approximately 4 tablespoons)

3 12-ounce cans chicken broth

1 medium bell pepper, chopped

2 medium onions, chopped

3 ribs celery, chopped

1 can cream of mushroom soup

1 8-ounce can tomato sauce

$\frac{1}{2}$ cup water

1 tablespoon parsley flakes

1 teaspoon Accent

3 cloves garlic, chopped

Salt and pepper to taste

$\frac{1}{4}$ teaspoon sweet basil

$\frac{1}{4}$ teaspoon poultry seasoning

1 teaspoon Worcestershire sauce

1 teaspoon lemon juice

2 pounds crawfish tails (thawed)

$\frac{1}{2}$ cup green onion tops, chopped

Mix flour and oil together to make roux. Put over medium heat and stir constantly until brown.

In a heavy Dutch oven, add all ingredients except crawfish and green onions. Let cook until vegetables are tender. Add roux and let cook for 30 minutes over medium heat. Add crawfish and green onions and cook for 10 minutes longer. Do not over-cook after adding crawfish.

Serve over hot bed of rice.

Leesville Café

Leesville residents discuss the issues of the day over lunch at the Leesville Cafe, listen to poetry over coffee at Joe Red's, pick up trinkets at Russell's Gift Shop, or learn gymnastics at Tumble Town USA. Third Street, with its new coat of blacktop, shows the activity of revitalization in a downtown where people gather, shop, and learn the area's history.

Incorporated in 1900, Leesville is located in the heart of Vernon Parish. Known as the "Wildflower Capital of Louisiana," Vernon Parish was established in 1871, but the first land grant was recorded in 1787. By 1880, the lumber industry had established a firm foothold in the area, but the timber was depleted by the time of the Great Depression, further exacerbating local economic conditions.

The local economy sprang back to life when Camp Polk was opened in 1941. Named for the Right Rev. Leonidas Polk, an Episcopal bishop more popularly known as "The Fighting Bishop" during the Civil War, Camp Polk went though a series of openings and closings. It has remained open since 1961 as Fort Polk.

Recently, Vernon Bank in Leesville had the 1960s-era facade stripped off of its downtown branch, exposing its original 1907 front, including a column made with marble from France. Inside, a drop ceiling was removed, exposing the original tin ceiling, and a balcony was opened up.

The Museum of the West, housed in the old Leesville Kansas City Southern Railroad Depot and surrounding land, preserves the history of the parish with a collection that includes logging implements, railroad memorabilia, and paintings by German prisoners of war from World War II.

Leesville boasts some famous daughters: Joan Blondell, who appeared in the Ziegfield Follies and several Broadway shows and movies, including 10 movies with Dick Powell (whom she married in 1936), lived with her family as a teenager in Leesville in the 1920s. Carolyn Leach Huntoon, the only woman to head the Johnson Space Center (1994–96), was born and raised in Leesville.

Take a stroll along Third Street in Leesville and encounter the charm of a historic small-town downtown area by visiting the Leesville Café.

Leesville Café

114 South Third Street

Leesville, Louisiana 71446

(337) 392-2651

182

SLOW-ROASTED BRISKET

Serves 6–10

1 7–10 pound brisket, well trimmed
1 envelope Knorr® onion soup mix
Ground black, red, and white peppers
Texjoy® steak seasoning

Wash and dry brisket. Generously season brisket with onion soup mix, ground black, red, and white peppers and steak seasoning.

Place brisket in baking pan, cover with heavy-duty aluminum foil and marinate in the refrigerator for two days.

Remove from the refrigerator and place the brisket in a 300-degree preheated oven for 30 minutes. Lower oven temperature to 250 degrees and bake for 5–6 hours.

Pan drippings/juices combined with cooked rice complete this entrée.

CAFÉ CLASSIC CHICKEN SALAD

Serves 6

6 whole chicken breasts

1 whole yellow onion

2 stalks celery

1 cup celery, finely chopped

$1/2$ cup green onions, finely chopped

$1/3$ cup yellow onions, finely chopped

$1/4$ cup fresh flat leaf parsley, chopped

$3/4$–1 cup mayonnaise

$1/4$ cup Dijon mustard

1–1 $1/2$ teaspoons salt

1 teaspoon white pepper

Iceberg, red, and green leaf lettuces (shredded)

Fresh fruit such as seedless grapes, strawberries or apples

Place chicken breasts, whole onion, and stalks of celery in pot and cover with water. Boil chicken until tender.

Remove chicken and refrigerate until cool. Reserve stock for another use. When chicken has cooled, remove skin and bones. Chop breast meat into a large dice.

Combine the chicken, celery, green onions, yellow onion, flat leaf parsley, mayonnaise, mustard, salt, and white pepper. Mix well and chill before serving.

To serve, place whole leaves of green leaf lettuce on chilled plates. Top this with a combination of shredded lettuces. Mound one cup of chicken salad onto lettuce beds. Garnish with fresh fruit: seedless grapes, strawberries, etc.

> *"I feel a recipe is only a theme, which an intelligent cook can play each time with a variation."*
> Madame Benoit

POOR MAN'S FILET

Serves 4

2 pounds ground chuck

1/4 cup green onion, minced

1/4 cup yellow onion, minced

1 clove garlic, minced

2 tablespoons Worcestershire sauce

Dash of hot sauce

1 tablespoon fresh flat leaf parsley, chopped

1 large egg, beaten

1 1/2 teaspoons salt

1/2 teaspoon black pepper

Dash of red pepper

Dash of white pepper

4–8 slices uncooked bacon

Combine all ingredients except the bacon in a large bowl. When well combined, shape into 4 round burgers. Wrap 1 or 2 slices of bacon around each burger, securing with toothpicks. Grill or bake the burgers until fully cooked.

In a separate saucepan, heat 1 cup of meat drippings (or beef stock) with ¾ cup butter and 2 tablespoons Worcestershire sauce and a dash of hot sauce. Remove toothpicks, cover burgers with sauce and serve.

Antique Rose Ville

Antique Rose Ville

2007 Freyou Road

New Iberia, Louisiana 70560

(337) 367-3000

www.antiqueroseville.com

The home occupied by Antique Rose Ville's restaurant and tea room is known as the Renoudet Cottage, named for its twentieth-century owners. One of Iberia Parish's oldest homes, it dates back to 1840, when it was owned by a Picard family. It was later occupied by William Weeks II (son of David Weeks, builder of Shadows on the Teche), and was used at other times to house the overseers of the Weeks family's plantations.

The Renoudet Cottage was moved in December of 1995 from its original site on St. Peter Street to its present location on Freyou Road. There, proprietor Linda D. Freyou and her husband, Simon, meticulously restored the home to its original condition.

The Renoudet Cottage is the second home the Freyous have restored. Their present home, Anastasia, was built in 1904. It sits alongside Antique Rose Ville and was moved to Freyou Road after being transported 50 miles by barge down the Intracoastal Canal from Berwick, Louisiana.

The grounds of Antique Rose Ville include four acres that have been uniquely designed for aesthetic enjoyment and pleasure. There are over 100 varieties of antique roses planted around the home and pond. Native plants surround the pond, including cypress trees and Louisiana irises. A working European-design lattice bridge, constructed by Simon, crosses the pond.

Fresh herbs from the grounds of Antique Rose Ville are used in Linda's cooking, and all meals are prepared with the freshest ingredients.

The origin of the name, Antique Rose Ville, is two-fold. As a young child, Linda played among the fragrant antique roses that grew on the trellises and dotted the landscape at her grandparents' homes. Later in life, she began collecting a certain type of antique pottery depicting flora native to North America. The pottery is known as Roseville—hence the name, Antique Rose Ville.

Antique Rose Ville's open pavilion area is located directly behind the Renoudet Cottage. It is made of old virgin cypress planks, windows, and doors from old homes and barns throughout the Acadiana region. The pavilion is connected to Au Jardin, which is designed for large groups.

HOMEMADE BROWNIES

Yields 16–20 brownies

¹/₂ cup butter

1 cup sugar

2 eggs

3 tablespoons cocoa

1 teaspoon baking powder

¹/₂ teaspoon salt

1 cup flour

¹/₂ teaspoon vanilla

Combine all ingredients. Pour into 9-inch square pan. Bake in oven at 350 degrees for 35 minutes.

187

POUND CAKE

1 cup butter
$^1/_2$ cup shortening
3 cups sugar
3 cups flour
1 cup evaporated milk
1 teaspoon vanilla
6 eggs

Cream butter, shortening, and sugar until fluffy. Add remaining ingredients, except for eggs. Then add eggs one at a time.

Grease tube pan and flour. Pour in batter.

Bake in preheated 325-degree oven for 1½ hours.

> *"There is no love sincerer than the love of food."*
> George Bernard Shaw

OLD-FASHIONED BUTTER COOKIES

Yields 6–7 dozen

3 cups sifted all-purpose flour

1 teaspoon baking powder

$^1/_2$ teaspoon salt

1 cup butter

$^3/_4$ cup sugar

1 egg

2 teaspoons cream

1 $^1/_2$ teaspoons vanilla

Sift flour with baking powder and salt. In a separate bowl, cream butter. Gradually add sugar, creaming well. Stir in egg, cream, and vanilla. Add dry ingredients. Mix well and chill ½ hour.

Roll out ⅓ of the dough at a time to ⅛-inch thickness on floured surface. Cut into desired shapes. Place on ungreased cookie sheets.

Bake at 400 degrees for 5–8 minutes.

Clementine Dining and Spirits

Clementine Dining and Spirits

113 E Main Street

New Iberia, Louisiana 70560

(337) 560-1007

The first thing one notices upon entering Clementine's is that the bar looks old. In fact, it was originally built in the 1890s out of tiger oak and mahogany somewhere in California. It was shipped to Loreauville, Louisiana, in the 1920s where it was Mr. Richard Provost's bar until the mid-1930s. It was then shipped down the bayou to its current location. His bar—Provost's on Main Street in New Iberia—remained open until the 1980s.

After Provost's closed, the building was left vacant and run-down for years. Mr. Cam Mestayer purchased the building and brought it back to life, opening a restaurant named Armand's. Armand's closed and Clementine took over in 1999.

The restaurant is now housed in two adjoining buildings. The main dining room has housed a variety of businesses in its long history, most recently serving as a dry cleaner's and barbershop.

The Clementine story itself dates back to the late 1800s. The restaurant was named Clementine Dining & Spirits to pay tribute to owner Wayne Peltier's favorite artist, Clementine Hunter. Clementine, a folk artist, was born in 1887 in the Cane River country of Louisiana. While in her fifties and working at Melrose Plantation, Clementine found tubes of paint lying around, thus beginning her life as an artist.

Clementine would paint on whatever she could find. Her first painting was rendered on a window shade. Her paintings came from daily life on Melrose Plantation— baptisms, funerals, washdays, and the harvesting of sugar cane are a few events that she documented. Clementine Hunter died in 1988 at the age of 101.

The restaurant incorporated Clementine's famous backwards-C-and-H insignia into its logo and the placement of its silverware. As the story goes, Clementine thought the normal C was rude, with its back to you, so she signed her C backwards with its arms reaching out to hug you.

A Clementine Hunter painting is prominently displayed near the turn-of-the-century mahogany bar and local artists are showcased throughout the restaurant.

FRIED GREEN TOMATOES

Serves 4

12–14 green tomato slices
½ pound claw crabmeat
4 tablespoons green onions, diced
1 cup brandy
1 cup seafood stock
4 teaspoons butter
2 eggs
2 cups milk
2 cups flour, seasoned to taste
Oil for frying

Combine eggs and milk in an open bowl. Dredge tomato slices through egg and milk mixture then batter with seasoned flour. In a skillet, heat oil and fry tomatoes until golden.

In another skillet, sauté green onions, crabmeat, and butter for about one minute. Add brandy to skillet and flame. Then add seafood stock and simmer for one more minute.

To plate, layer tomato and crabmeat and drizzle top with remaining sauce.

ROASTED RED PEPPER AND WILD MUSHROOM BISQUE WITH CRAB

Serves 5

4 tablespoons butter

¹/₂ large yellow onion, finely diced

¹/₂ tablespoon garlic, minced

10 shiitake mushrooms, sliced

2–3 Portobello mushrooms, chopped

5 dried morels, rehydrated and sliced
 (button mushrooms can be substituted)

4 red peppers, roasted and puréed

1 cup water (reserved from Morels)

1 quart heavy cream

¹/₂ quart half-and-half

1 teaspoon dried thyme

1 teaspoon granulated garlic

1 bay leaf

1 tablespoon crab base (or seafood stock)

¹/₂ tablespoon chicken base

Sweat onion and garlic in butter. Add Shitake and Portobello mushrooms and sauté for 5 minutes. Add morels and pepper purée. When purée comes to a boil, add the reserved water, heavy cream, half-and-half, thyme, garlic, and bay leaves. Simmer for 10 minutes, and then add bases. Stir well and simmer for 10 more minutes. Thicken with Blonde Roux if desired.

PORTOBELLO PIZZA

Serves 4

4 large Portobello mushrooms
2 tablespoons shallots, diced
2 tablespoons olive oil
1 tablespoon garlic, minced
1 pound shrimp or crabmeat
2 cups mozzarella cheese
1 cup prepared marinara sauce for plating
Parsley, chopped (for garnish)

Italian Vinaigrette Marinade

$^1/_2$ cup olive oil
1 tablespoon red wine vinegar
1 tablespoon lemon juice
$^1/_2$ tablespoon Dijon Mustard
$^1/_2$ teaspoon dried oregano
$^1/_2$ teaspoon dried thyme
$^1/_2$ teaspoon dried rosemary

Mix the vinaigrette ingredients. Marinate Portobello mushrooms in Italian Vinaigrette for 2 hours. Grill for 1 minute on each side.

In a skillet, sauté shallots, olive oil, garlic, and shrimp or crabmeat until cooked. Top each Portobello with sautéed crab or shrimp and mozzarella cheese. Place on a baking sheet and bake at 400 degrees for 5–7 minutes or until cheese is melted.

Ladle marinara onto 4 plates and spread to make a thin layer. Place Portobello Pizza on top of marinara. Garnish with parsley. Serve with garlic bread.

TUNA AU POIVRE

Serves 4

4 8-ounce tuna steaks (Sashimi grade)
Kosher salt (to taste)
Cracked black pepper (to taste)
$^1/_2$ cup brandy
1 cup heavy cream
$^1/_4$ cup green onions, chopped
Olive oil
Chopped parsley (for garnish)

Coat the bottom of a heated skillet with olive oil. Season tuna with salt and pepper and sear in skillet for 1 minute on each side. Remove from skillet and keep warm.

Deglaze hot skillet with brandy, then add green onions. When brandy is reduced almost completely, add heavy cream and reduce to desired consistency. Ladle sauce over tuna. Garnish with chopped parsley.

193

Nash's

Nash's

101 E 2nd Street

Broussard, Louisiana 70518

(337) 839-9333

www.nashsrestaurant.com

The area now known as Broussard was originally named Cote Gelee (Frozen Hills) because of its hilly ridge area and the severe winter of 1784. The town was formally founded in 1884 and was named after Valsin Broussard, a prominent local merchant, who formed the first Vigilante Committee after the robbery of his own store. He was also a direct descendant of Joseph Gaurhept Broussard de Beau Soleil, one of the first 200 Acadians to arrive in Louisiana on February 27, 1765, aboard the Santo Domingo.

After the Acadians arrived, Frenchmen fleeing the turmoil of the French Revolution also flocked to the area. Other ethnic groups began to arrive as well, including people fleeing the slave revolts in Santo Domingo and Haiti. Life was hard in the area, and the success of farming depended upon the difficult task of transporting produce across the Atchafalaya Swamp to markets in New Orleans. Cotton was the major crop, with sugar cane rapidly gaining popularity.

The completion of the railroad from New Orleans to Morgan City just before the Civil War was a major catalyst to farming and business interests in the area. Even today, trains running from coast to coast still pass through Broussard.

As the boll weevil ravaged cotton crops, Broussard's primary agricultural crop became sugarcane. Soybean and hay production, as well as horse and cattle farming, are now also prominent. The principal industries are oil and gas service companies, food distributors, real estate developments, and manufacturing.

Broussard has gone from a horse-and-buggy community, with large sugarcane plantation homes, to a current-day industrial community with over 300 businesses. Yet one still experiences the town's historic charm through the atmosphere of elegant dining. Creole home cooking and Cajun food are available at several local restaurants. Nash's is located in one of the oldest homes in the area.

GRILLED EGGPLANT, TOMATO, FRESH MOZZARELLA, PORTOBELLO MUSHROOMS, AND FRESH BASIL SALAD

Serves 3

3 pieces eggplant, sliced ¼-inch thick
   with skin on
3 pieces vine-ripe or Creole tomatoes,
   sliced ¼-inch thick
3 pieces Portobello mushrooms,
   sliced ¼-inch thick
3 pieces fresh Mozzarella cheese,
   sliced ¼-inch thick
2 tablespoons fresh basil leaves, finely chopped
2 cups freshly-grown spring mix
Extra-virgin olive oil
Balsamic vinegar

Coat a sauté pan with a thin layer of extra-virgin olive oil. Salt and pepper eggplant, tomatoes, and Portobello mushrooms. Grill all three vegetables in the same sauté pan on both sides.

Remove from sauté pan and place on dry paper towel to dry.

Place spring mix on a platter. Layer each vegetable and slices of fresh Mozzarella cheese. Sprinkle balsamic vinegar and fresh sweet basil on top.

Options: You can add grilled chicken, duck breast, or fish to this salad. A vinaigrette dressing, such as balsamic or raspberry, will complement this dish.

SHRIMP AND WHITE BEANS

Serves 4

Beans

1 pound dried great northern beans

$\frac{1}{2}$ pound ham or seasoned meat

1 tablespoon margarine

1 medium onion, finely chopped

$\frac{1}{2}$ medium bell pepper, chopped

4 ribs celery, chopped

8–10 cups of water

1 cup chicken broth

1 tablespoon fresh parsley, chopped

Salt and pepper to taste

In a stockpot, sauté margarine, meat, seasoning, and garlic. Add chicken broth and beans. Add 8–10 cups water. Let cook for two hours, until beans are tender.

Add parsley, salt, and pepper to taste last. If necessary, add water while cooking.

Shrimp

1 tablespoon unsalted butter

$\frac{1}{2}$ teaspoon fresh chopped garlic

8 ounces peeled shrimp (size optional)

2 ounces shrimp stock

2 ounces green onions, chopped

After the beans are cooked, sauté all ingredients and let simmer until the shrimp are cooked. Add 8 ounces of the cooked white beans and simmer again until heated, stirring occasionally.

Pour over steamed rice and serve.

> **"I hate people who are not serious about their meals."**
> Oscar Wilde

SHRIMP AND CORN BISQUE

Serves 8

1 cup unsalted butter

1 cup bleached all-purpose flour

1 gallon shrimp stock

3 pounds medium-sized shrimp

2 #303 cans whole kernel corn or creamed corn

2 cups heavy cream

2 cups onion, finely chopped

1 cup celery, finely chopped

$\frac{1}{2}$ red pepper, diced

2 tablespoons granulated garlic

1 tablespoon fresh thyme, chopped

1 tablespoon fresh tarragon, chopped

3 bay leaves

1 teaspoon granulated white pepper

1 tablespoon fresh parsley, chopped

Peel and devein shrimp, saving peelings for stock. Boil shrimp in plain water and drain. Set aside.

Boil shrimp peelings to make a stock. Use 1¼ gallons of water so that you have enough stock for your bisque. Strain and set aside.

In a stockpot, melt butter and add flour. Stir to make a white roux (10 minutes). Add 1 gallon of shrimp stock. Let come to a boil.

Add heavy cream, corn, onion, celery, peppers, thyme, white pepper, garlic, and bay leaves. Let come to a boil.

Add 3 pounds of cooked shrimp. Let come to a boil. Let cook for 30 minutes after boiling.

Add chopped tarragon and chopped parsley.

Pujo Street Café

Pujo Street Café

901 Ryan Street

Lake Charles, Louisiana 70601

(337) 439-2054

www.pujostreet.com

Lake Charles was first inhabited by Native American Indians. They named what is now the Rio Hondo river—which flows through town—Quelqueshue, meaning "crying eagle." Later, this name would be modified and the surrounding parish christened Calcasieu.

Europeans arrived in the area in the 1760s. Their main interests were the dense pine forests and the waterway. Legend has it that the pirate Jean Lafitte was a frequent visitor to the area before and after the War of 1812. He had established his own "kingdom" of Barataria in the swamps and bayous near New Orleans after the Louisiana Purchase of 1803. His army fought alongside Andrew Jackson in resisting the British attack on New Orleans.

One of the earliest recorded settlers to the area was Charles Sallier, who built a home on the shell beach where Lake Charles now stands. Later, the area was given the name "Charlie's Lake." When the city was finally incorporated, the formal name Charleston was taken from the informal "Charles Town."

Trade on the waterways and the burgeoning lumber industry propelled the area to massive growth, prompting Louisiana's government to move the parish seat to Lake Charles from its former location at Marion, eight miles upriver. The parish courthouse and jail were also moved by barge to Lake Charles, which was still called Charleston. Six years later, the town was renamed Lake Charles to reflect its heritage.

By the time of the Civil War, attitudes toward slavery in the area were mixed. Less than five percent of the population were slaves, and involvement in the war was limited. After the war, Lake Charles' lumber industry thrived. The area's mills were swamped with orders and the population exploded. By the 1890s, finer homes were being built.

In 1898, Gordon's Drug Store was built at 901 Ryan Street, with the upstairs serving as doctors' offices. Four years later, in a move that would ultimately save the building from destruction, brick was added to the structure. The Great Fire of 1910 destroyed most of downtown Lake Charles, but this building was spared, making it one of the few surviving structures from the pre-1910 era.

REDFISH MEUNIÈRE

Serves 1

1 8-ounce redfish fillet

Flour to coat

2 tablespoons butter

Sauce

2 tablespoons white wine

1 teaspoon garlic, minced

1 teaspoon parsley, chopped

2 lemon slices

1 teaspoon Worcestershire sauce

1 tablespoon butter

Lightly dust fillet with flour and sauté in butter until cooked, browning on both sides. Place fish on a warm plate.

Empty excess liquid from pan. Deglaze with white wine. Add garlic, parsley, and lemon slices. Sauté for just a minute, then add Worchestershire sauce and reduce by half. Remove from heat, add butter, and swirl pan until incorporated.

Pour over fillet as a sauce.

BREAD PUDDING WITH RUM SAUCE

Serves 12

15 ounces white sandwich bread

2 ½ cups sugar

5 eggs

3 ½ cups skim milk

2 tablespoons vanilla

Tear bread slices into small pieces and place in a large bowl. Add remaining ingredients and stir until well mixed.

Coat a 9-inch by 13-inch pan and pour mixture in. Let come to room temperature about 45 minutes.

Preheat oven to 350 degrees. Bake for 45 minutes or until puffed up and golden brown. Let stand for 30 minutes before slicing. Serve with rum sauce (recipe follows).

Rum Sauce

½ cup butter

1 cup sugar

1 egg

¼ cup white rum

Cream butter and sugar in mixer at high speed until light and creamy. At low speed, add egg and mix until blended. Add rum and mix until blended. Mix on high for 20–30 minutes until light and fluffy.

Serve atop the bread pudding.

"Dinner, a time when ... one should eat wisely but not too well, and talk well but not too wisely."
W. Somerset Maugham

OYSTERS PUJO

Serves 8

1/2 teaspoon olive oil

1/2 tablespoon garlic, minced

1/2 tablespoon shallot, minced

3/4 cup tasso (highly seasoned smoked pork), minced

3/4 cup smoked Gouda, minced

4 cups fresh spinach

2 ounces Southern Comfort

1/2 cup heavy whipping cream

8 large oysters

Flour

Buttermilk

1 cup pecan pieces

1 cup Panko breadcrumbs

Oil

Sauté garlic, shallots, and tasso in olive oil over high heat for about 3 minutes. Add Gouda, cooking another 3 minutes. Then add spinach and wilt down.

Deglaze with Southern Comfort and add cream. Reduce by half and set aside.

In a food processor, make a coating mixture with the pecans and Panko breadcrumbs.

Dust the oysters with flour, dip in buttermilk, and roll in coating mixture. Fry oysters until crispy, then place in shells, topping with sauce mixture.

Bake for 5–7 minutes at 400 degrees or until golden brown.

Serve on a bed of greens with a lemon garnish.

Acknowledgments

Many hands and hearts have helped to shape this book. We must first thank the chefs of Louisiana for sharing their talents, recipes, and stories. Eva, the concierge at the Hotel Monteleone—what would we do without you? The folks at the Hotel Maison de Ville and the Audubon Cottages—all we can say is that everyone in America should stay at one of those cottages for sheer ecstasy.

We heartily support historic preservation. Almost one year ago when we started this book, who would have foreseen the outcome? Just five days before Hurricane Katrina, we traveled throughout the state taking photographs, making friends, enjoying the music, and, most of all, loving every single bite. We were cruising on the Baltic Sea and watched in horror as we saw the devastation of the storm and prayed fervently for those in peril. Coming home, we were filled with sadness at the aftermath, but our noble publisher, Rue Judd, generously, volunteered to donate a portion of the proceeds of this book to the National Trust Hurricane Recovery Fund. This allowed us, in some small way, to be able to help in the recovery process. Also, we are grateful for the incomparable efforts of the staff at Bright Sky Press, Carol, Haley, and Isabel.

An April publication date seemed like a miraculous endeavor, but the restaurants, hotels, and plantations that we were able to reach were supportive even in their time of tremendous torment. Many said that such a book would help them to publicize their restaurants to travelers at just the time that they would be ready for business.

This travel guide and cookbook is also a way for others throughout the country to lovingly savor a piece of Louisiana history, explore its unique culinary style, and ignite their desire to, as Louisiana's motto says, "Come as you are. Leave Different."

Index

R

Raspberry Coulis 89
Ratatouille 84
Ravigote Sauce 92
Red Beans and Sausage, Lasyone's 180
Redfish and Shrimp Chupe 125
Redfish Meunière 199
Remoulade Sauce, Bon Ton Café 120
Remoulade Sauce, Tujague's 76
Rib-Eye, Barbecue 64
Rice, Bouillon 119
Rice, Lasyone's Dirty 180
Roast Duck 97
Roast Duck and Andouille Pasta 177
Roasted Red Pepper and Wild Mushroom Bisque with Crab 192
Rosarita Margarita 52
Rum Raisin Crème Anglaise 65
Rum Sauce 200

S

Salmon, Chili and Cumin-Rubbed 167
Scalloped Potatoes 170
Seafood Okra Gumbo 60
Scalloped Potatoes 170
Shrimp and Andouille-Stuffed Quail 151
Shrimp and Corn Bisque 197
Shrimp and Tomato Smoked Marinara 61
Shrimp and White Beans 196
Shrimp, Barbecued 81
Shrimp, Fire-Roasted 72
Shrimp, Muriel's Barbecue 57
Shrimp Toulouse 88
Slaw, Midori Mango 100
Slow-Cooked Lamb Shanks, Carrots, Turnips, and Shallots 141
Slow-Roasted Brisket 183
Snapper, Whole-Roasted B-Line 100
Sour Cream Pound Cake 25
Spicy Butter Sauce 57
Spiced Butternut Squash Soup 167
Steak, Bronzed 33

Strawberry Balsamico Jam 80
Strawberry Balsamico Swirled Cheesecake 80
Strawn's Pie Crust 170
Sugar-Free Cheesecakes 104
Sweet Potato, Shrimp, and Corn Bisque 47
Sweet Potatoes, Mashed 99

T

Tomato and Goat Cheese Salad 175
Tenderloin of Beef a la Cruz 133
Trout Meunière Amandine 112
Tuna Au Poivre 193
Turtle Soup, Commander's Palace 136
Turtle Soup, Galatoire's 111
Turtle Soup, The Cabin 161

V

Voodoo Oysters 174

W

Whipped Cream 117
Whiskey Sauce 93
White Beans 165
White Chocolate Ganache 89
Whole Roasted B-Line Snapper 100

Y

Yam and Pecan Pie 162

Photo Credits

Photographs by Steve Bauer
23, 41, 42, 47, 55, 57, 77, 84, 87, 106, 107, 121,147, 151, 155, 161, 165, 166, 169, 173 (top), 179, 183, 187, 188, 191, 192, 195, 199, 201

Photographs by Louisiana Office of Tourism
1, 8, 9 (bottom), 10, 11 (bottom left), 12, 13 (top right), 14 (bottom right), 15, 17 (left), 18 (right), 21, 26, 32, 35, 38, 59, 71, 89, 97, 109, 142, 143, 146, 149, 150, 153, 154, 157, 158, 159, 163, 173 (bottom), 175, 181, 203

Photographs by New Orleans CVB / Harry Costner
56

Photographs by New Orleans CVB / Richard Nowitz
Front cover, back cover, 2, 17 (right), 19, 45, 96, 101, 134, 135, 145, 208

Photographs by New Orleans CVB / Ann Purcell
14 (top left)

Photographs by New Orleans CVB / Carl Purcell
14 (bottom left and top right), 25, 88

Photographs by New Orleans CVB / Jeff Strout
11 (top), 18 (left)

Photographs by Donn Young Photography
6, 11 (bottom right), 13 (top left and bottom)

Photographs courtesy the restaurant
9 (top), 29, 30, 31, 36, 37, 39, 50, 51, 52, 63, 64, 65, 67, 73, 79, 80, 83, 85, 90, 91, 95, 99, 103, 104, 111, 113, 115, 116, 123, 124, 128, 131, 132, 139, 141, 177